RESCUED

A PRODIGAL'S JOURNEY HOME

OTHER BOOKS AND AUDIO BOOKS
BY JERRY EARL JOHNSTON:

A Woman's Worth

Dads and Other Heroes

RESCUED

A PRODIGAL'S JOURNEY HOME

JERRY EARL JOHNSTON

Covenant Communications, Inc.

For the grandkids—
a manual for what not to do and how not to do it.

ACKNOWLEDGMENTS

I'VE GOTTEN A GREAT DEAL of support as a journalist and a writer. My family has been patient and positive. So have my editors—Kathy Jenkins and Kirk Shaw at Covenant Communications . . . not to mention the *Deseret News* editors who have always given me plenty of rope to hang myself. I need to thank James Ferrell and my buddy Luis Casas for convincing me this was the book I really needed to write. Others who deserve my thanks play out their contributions in these pages.

I also need to single out my wife, Carol. She has not only hung in there with me, but has also often kept me from spinning off the planet. Whatever prompts women like her to stick with needy souls like me is one of the mysteries where I never dabble.

Jerry Earl Johnston
Brigham City, May 2011

CONTENTS

FOREWORD

THIS IS A BOOK YOU will read once—all at once—in one sitting. It reads as swiftly as one of Jerry's columns but moves as deeply as an ocean current. I began by scribbling down quotes that I wanted to remember. Before long, I didn't want to interrupt the arc of the story even to memorialize a thought. I read it on a computer screen before it had gone to an editor. I remember thinking, *I wouldn't change a word.*

I have been inspired over the years by tales of great achievement. But I am changed only by a different kind of story: by accounts of deep failure. Why? Because achievements congratulate man while failures necessitate God. Small men can tell of their successes (and most do). My soul is invited heavenward only by those whose honesty is large enough to share with us their mistakes. I'm speaking now not primarily of outward mistakes, as a person can rattle off behavioral transgressions in ways that border on bragging. But when I hear a man tell how his heart became hardened, how his thoughts darkened, and how, losing all bearings, he turned from his faith, I encounter a meekness that can finally invite me to give up the cramped tales I have been spinning about myself.

At the level of our hearts, all are guilty. The only question is whether we will be honest enough both to see and to admit it. It is our answer to this question that determines whether our lives end in heartbreak or, as Jerry's has, in a heart that is broken enough to be healed. Jerry remains, of course, very much alive, for which I and all his other friends and readers are grateful. And I am grateful to him for writing a book that will help me to live my own life better— more honestly, more joyfully, more contentedly. I am grateful that although he is a man of achievement, his story is rather a story of God's achievement—how the Lord healed a heart that had stopped working as it needed to if Jerry (and, by extension, us) was to survive in this life and enjoy what awaited him in the next.

"Howbeit for this cause I obtained mercy," Paul wrote to Timothy (1 Tim. 1:16), "that in me . . . Jesus Christ might shew forth all longsuffering, for a pattern to them which should hereafter believe on him to life everlasting." The apostle Paul could have been describing Jerry's story as well as his own. By confessing his struggles to us, Jerry, like Paul, has allowed us to see the power of God unto redemption and to see that this is a process that is available to us as well. More than a story, the book is a confession. Because of this, it points us to Christ rather than to the author, which ends up making it a tale of the only kind of success that really matters.

"God was closing in," Jerry writes in his tight and compelling prose. And so He was. And is. The reader is witness to how His never giving up on Jerry is but an instance of His never giving up at all.

On anyone.

—James L. Ferrell, author of *The Peacegiver*

All the firstborn of thy sons thou shalt redeem.
And none shall appear before me empty.

—Exodus 34:20

CHAPTER ONE:
A Wedding Cake in the Rain

While I write this, I keep looking out the window where the late evening clouds are as hard and gray as Grandma's old pewter dishes. Rain has speckled the window, and an evergreen the size of the National Christmas Tree blocks my view of the world.

And yet, I can still see the Polar Star.

That's because, tonight, the Polar Star is down inside of me.

Such isn't always the case. And for many years in my life, it was never the case.

But now, when I need a guiding light, I can often find it within.

That's just one of the blessings that comes with returning to a life of faith.

I'm a classic prodigal son. And being a prodigal son puts me in league with a rather ragtag group of folks. There's that fellow in the parable who buries his talent in the ground instead of putting it to good use, not to mention any nitwit dim enough to light a candle and cover it with a bushel basket.

But the sin for all three of us is the same. Prodigals, talent hoarders, and light hiders are given the most joyous gifts God has to offer, but we make bad use of them.

Some bury those gifts and hide them, others shield them from those in need. But prodigals are the most devious of the three. We take God's wonderful spiritual riches and spend them on ourselves. Contrary to popular belief, *prodigal* doesn't mean "wayward." It means "extravagant," as in "careless and wasteful with the precious things of the kingdom."

The nice thing is we prodigals get a chance to make things right.

That's the theme of this book. It is about my life in the kingdom (the gospel), my drift into extravagant selfishness, and my ultimate attempt to turn things around. Or, I should say, God's attempt to turn things around. The only spiritual memoirs worth their salt, I've found, are never about people but about God working marvels in the lives of people—especially stubborn people.

And my stubbornness has taken a toll. I am sixty-two now, but nobody tells me I look fifty-two or even that I'm a "young sixty-two."

That's because flattery, to be believed, must contain a smidgen of truth. And my face has obviously logged many needless miles. Oh, I'm not yet in cahoots with poet W. H. Auden, who said his face resembled "a wedding cake left out in the rain." But my countenance is growing as woeful as Quixote's. My face is a road map of the many byways I've traveled—most of them leading to dead ends.

When you're a prodigal son, you get around. And like the author of the hymn "Come Thou Fount of Every Blessing," I have been "prone to wander."

In that respect, this book is my travelogue. This isn't "the road not taken," it's the road taken. And it's a cautionary tale to all those who are tempted to follow in my footsteps.

My story, you'll find, has many nouns in it—a lot of people, places, things, and ideas. Bolivia, Mexico, Montana, and Utah all show up here. As do several leaders of the LDS Church, some former teachers, hockey players, flight attendants, Bob Dylan, Shakespeare, cab drivers, C. S. Lewis, and more than a few salt-of-the-earth Latter-day Saints.

There's a young man and an old man, a person of faith and a fool, a seeker, a finder, a loser—and those are just the roles I play in the book.

Don't worry. I've put in plenty of markers and road signs so you'll know where you are in my life—something I seldom knew as I was living it.

As for the passing years, I've found I tend to live them out in well-measured chunks. About forty years ago I was an LDS missionary in Bolivia. That is here.

Some twenty years ago I returned to the Church after spending twenty years as a post-mission apostate. That's here as well.

But the one event that pulls everything together—the drawstring that serves to cinch up the splayed corners of my life—happened in the year 2000 when the *Deseret News* sent me to Bolivia to cover President Gordon B. Hinckley's dedication of the Cochabamba temple. It was both a moment of truth and a moment for truth. Looking back, I can see my life pivoting on that return trip to Bolivia like an angel on the head of a pin.

And that return trip to Bolivia, as the old-time radio announcers would say, is where our story begins.

CHAPTER TWO:

Sugar on a Bowl of Jewels

LA PAZ, BOLIVIA, IS A city that will take your breath away.

And I mean that literally.

At 12,000 feet above sea level, the place is rich in culture but poor in oxygen. Talking and walking at the same time makes you pant. Running to catch a bus or a plane can send you into cardiac arrest.

But now I'm getting way ahead of my story.

From 1968 to 1970 I served an LDS mission in Bolivia. And as I mentioned earlier, exactly thirty years later—the year 2000—I was headed back there as a newspaper columnist for the *Deseret News*. LDS *Church News* editor, Gerry Avant, asked if I'd go down to cover President Gordon B. Hinckley's dedication of the Cochabamba temple. She thought I could add some context to the piece—punch it up a little.

She was about to get more than she bargained for.

La Paz, the capital city, would be my starting point. But then La Paz is the starting point for everything in Bolivia. Most third world capitals are like the sun with other towns spinning around them as planets. Small countries have room for only one grand city.

La Paz fills the bottom and sides of a great bowl rimmed by the Altiplano—the high plains of the Andes. Mount Illimani rises like Sinai on the far side of the bowl. At dusk, when the streetlights ignite, the snowy peak looks like a mound of sugar about to be spooned over a bowl of jewels.

I arrived at dusk on April 26, 2000.

The communists had yet to win control of Bolivia, though they were making a lot of noise. And in the United States the tragedies of 9-11 were just dark sparks in the minds of the terrorists. So, for the time being, the world was serenely spinning on its axis.

All was well.

For the time being.

I cleared customs quickly at the airport, hailed a cab, and began the slow, wobbly descent into the city on cobblestone streets. Sights and sounds, long lost to my memory, surfaced again like hibernating flowers. Old fears and longings came back to me. I wondered if what I felt was how it would feel to have the veil finally lifted and be shown the preexistence. It was both strange and familiar, invigorating and unnerving. And I was alive to the moment, focused, living on the surface of my skin as I did in my missionary days. I liked the feeling.

"I'm back in La Paz after thirty years," I told the cabby.

He carefully framed me in his rearview mirror.

"Very good," he said in crisp, clear Bolivian Spanish. "Welcome."

His car was a clunker, like most cars in Bolivia. The country had no seaport, so it relied on hand-me-downs from its neighbors—Chile, Peru, and Argentina.

As a missionary I always chatted up the cab drivers, hoping a personal connection would earn me a break on the fare. Usually the opposite happened. Getting to be buddies with the driver only made him bold enough to pad his price.

"I'm here for the dedication of the Mormon temple in Cochabamba," I said. "You know about the Mormons?"

Thirty years before nobody had heard of the Mormons. Now, I'd find everyone had heard of them. And everyone had an opinion—often a private opinion and a public opinion.

"Yes, I know the Mormons," the driver said. "The Church of Jesus Christ of Seventh Day Saints."

He seemed so proud of his information that I didn't bother to correct him.

"Good people, the Mormons," he went on—probably angling for a bigger tip. "A couple of your '*viejos*' live around here somewhere."

Viejos, I thought. Spanish for "old men." He meant the LDS missionaries.

"You mean the elders," I said.

"Yes," he said. "Los Elderes."

The city hadn't changed much, except for a dash of progress here and there. The squat, adobe huts were the same, but they all had house numbers now. Streets that before were alleyways now had names. The occasional Internet café came and went as we jiggled along. It was odd to think of Bolivians sitting in front of a computer screen watching *The Simpsons.*

"I'm at the Hotel Sagarnaga," I said. "You know where it is?"

"Yes," he said. "It's on Sagarnaga."

Sagarnaga turned out to be a jaunty little street running along the lower side of the bowl. I had vague memories of such streets from my former life in La Paz. The guidebook said folk musicians and artists hung out on Sagarnaga, along with the occasional pick-pocket. And a witch's market—complete with good-luck llama fetuses—was just a stone's throw away. I'd booked a hotel there so I could be near the city center.

As we edged along, the traffic tightened. We passed a couple of female traffic cops decked out in full makeup and fancy hair, like debutantes en route to the Policeman's Ball.

"We getting close?" I asked.

"Six or seven more blocks," he said. "I had to take a detour to get around the student protest."

"What are they protesting?"

"What they always protest," he said. "Injustice."

I would later learn they were looking for "water justice." Tomorrow it would be "rice justice." Injustice was a way of life in Bolivia. The law was worthless. It was all about who you knew. To get ahead you needed a "patron," a father figure who could open a few doors in exchange for undying loyalty. I think it must have been the same in Old Palestine, since so many in the Gospels seem intent on winning the favor of Jesus.

We arrived at the hotel ten or twelve blocks later.

And I was right.

The driver jacked up the fare we'd agreed on because of the protest. I huffed my own little protest over injustice then paid him.

The *Church News* had arranged for two American elders in the area to meet me at the hotel the next morning. They were to show me a splash of local color then take me to the station, where I'd catch a bus to Oruro, my favorite town as a missionary. After a day in Oruro, I'd go on to Cochabamba for the temple dedication.

The elders arrived early, well groomed and nervous. I could tell they weren't sure how important I was—or wasn't—and didn't know how much of the gritty side of the city I could stomach. I didn't have the heart to tell them very little grit got to me anymore. Over time I'd become jaded. I no longer felt shocked by sin and vice.

After taking me on a quick stroll down Sagarnaga, one elder said, "Let's visit the Gutierrez family."

I got the feeling that visiting the Gutierrez family was the default choice around here when you didn't know what else to do.

For me, it turned out to be a happy choice. I was in need of an emotional payday.

We dodged down a maze of identical shops just off Sagarnaga, stopping at a stack of bright blankets piled near a doorway. It was a textile shop. Soon, Sister Gutierrez emerged, dressed in a bowler hat and billowing skirts—the trademarks of her tribe. Brother Gutierrez, a 1940-style fedora squarely on his head, came from the shadows a moment later. We all pinched together in their store. It was about the size of a walk-in closet.

If it's true, as a professor once told me, that people can be sorted into just twenty-six types, I quickly realized I'd met Brother and Sister Gutierrez a hundred times as a missionary and maybe a thousand times since. They were leaven-in-the-loaf Christians. Outside their little shop, the world clattered and banged along. The smell of cheap liquor and cheap perfume filled the air, shady figures slid along the walls, but Brother and Sister Gutierrez had overcome the world. Their little store was as tranquil as a manger. It was a tiny lantern in the dark. And there was something about them that seemed almost transparent. Like the faces in Russian icon paintings, their faces held and cast no shadows. And I soaked my weary bones in the warm pool of their goodwill.

Brother Gutierrez had precious little education to muddy his relationship with the supernatural. And he had no social or economic status, no class distinction to protect. He could simply be himself. And the gospel had shown him his true self was selfless. Modern-day cynics have trouble believing that a person could be both authentic and giving. In fact, they assume do-gooders were the most egotistical of all.

Modern-day cynics haven't met Brother Gutierrez.

As we spoke, I found myself flashing back to my mission when a Pentecostal minister, Brother Vargas, had joined the Church. Becoming a Mormon deprived him of his career, so he set up shop as an untrained, freelance barber. His haircuts were the worst haircuts south of the Panama Canal. But my companion and I went to him for a trim every two weeks. So did other elders. That was when the fad of wearing hats first took root in our mission district.

But Brother Vargas had a heart like a golden apple.

And Brother and Sister Gutierrez seemed to have fallen from the same tree. I'm sure it would have embarrassed them to know how much I envied their natural goodness. I was too self-conscious of my own actions to ever achieve it. My education, for all its gifts, had also taken away my gift for unexamined spontaneity.

Sister Gutierrez, especially, found a place in my heart. She tended to look down when she spoke, like a nun practicing "custody of the eyes." She must have been fifty or so, but she seemed as light and alert as a young bird. She registered everything. As one novelist had put it, she was a person who seemed so sensitive she could be bruised by cotton swabs. And yet, she carried an inner resilience. One suspected, in a crisis, she could not only endure but would rise above whatever the world hurled her way. I saw that quality often in the women of Bolivia. The Indian men were often "quiet machos" while the women ran the show.

I've thought of the two of them many times since that day. I know, should I ever go back to La Paz, I could never find their shop again. It was one cell in a sprawling honeycomb. But that's okay. I didn't need to find their place. I took its sweetness with me when I left.

We chatted for a spell, then the elders began checking their watches and saying we had to get going. My bus awaited. Not much in Bolivia happened on time, except for bus and plane departures.

We went back to the hotel to get my bags, passing ads for McDonald's and Pizza Hut along the way—businesses unheard of here during my mission. A few years later the initiative of the owners of those franchises would be undercut by communism.

As I dawdled in La Paz, in fact, the Marxists were mounting protests in Cochabamba that would turn ugly and threaten to derail the temple dedication.

The Marxists always had a heyday in countries where people felt left out. They preached the gospel of Robin Hood—take from the rich, give to the poor. The problem was in countries like Bolivia, the rich were so few and the poor so many, everyone ended up with nothing.

In 1969, my companion and I had knocked on the door of a Marxist, the first one I'd ever met. He said we were kidding ourselves about religion and told us the United States was a giant octopus with tentacles in every country.

He was thinking about politics.

He should have been thinking business. The world was fast becoming a Burger King world.

"So you were here thirty years ago," one of the elders said as we watched for a cab. They were tipping to the fact I lacked the gravity of a real Church authority. I was just a guy on a mission, kind of like them.

"Tell me," he said, "what differences do you see in Bolivia?"

Over the next three days I would have conversations with several elders and sisters about "what was different" today in Bolivia from days gone by. And I'd always play up the thrilling days of yesteryear—the frontier years, the years of trailblazing.

Most conversations would go something like this:

Elder: What was Bolivia like back in the 1960s?

Me: Like this. The Church here is what's different now. Our mission had three countries in it—Bolivia, the southern part of Peru, and the northern part of Chile.

Elder: You're kidding.

Me: Nope. But you have to remember that was a long time ago. One of my first companions was Lorenzo Snow. Sometimes we'd go weeks down here without seeing another American. In fact, half the towns in Bolivia had never had a Mormon in them. There were no wards, no chapels. We did our baptizing in lakes and public swimming pools.

Elder: No way.

Me: It's the truth. There were only 350 members of the Church in Bolivia when I got here, and I met half of those at my first district conference in La Paz. How many members are there now?

Elder: I don't know. About 120,000, I think.

Me: That's what I figured. And my companions and I baptized most of those. Not an easy task when you consider we had to travel around the country on horseback.

It was all true.

Except for that last little bit about baptisms and horses.

And the Lorenzo Snow comment.

My itinerary in Bolivia was to be short, simple, and cheap. Funds were tight at the newspaper. I was to go to La Paz then Oruro then Cochabamba and then back to La Paz for one night before flying north to Miami, where I'd file my first story. The plan had so few moving parts I figured nothing could mess it up.

But then such are the schemes of mice and men.

My bus to Oruro turned out to be a luxury *flota*—a big-bodied affair with personal television sets and a "ride attendant" to keep us in treats. It was like the cabin of an airliner with tires where the wings should be. After boarding, we were soon up the side of the La Paz bowl and back on the flat Altiplano roaring along, the clouds hanging so low we seemed, indeed, to be airborne. I reached in my travel bag and grabbed a bottle of antacid. After a series of tests back home, two doctors had told me my chest pains had nothing to do with my heart.

"At some point, I have to believe the tests," one of them had said. He figured the pain was acid related.

As for my shortness of breath, I figured that had to be the altitude.

The ache in my arm had to be from sleeping funny.

We human beings, I've learned, can convince ourselves of anything.

We motored smoothly along, the heavy shock absorbers eating up the bumps. The Altiplano was rugged and worn, like the Aymara people who live there. The Incas had given up trying to conquer the Aymara. They were natural warriors. A great many Bolivian war heroes were Aymara. And the Aymara language is just as brutal—full of spit and explosions. We missionaries once had a member of our branch read the Christmas story in Aymara instead of Spanish. He lost his voice halfway through and couldn't speak. There is a reason Bolivian Indians are quiet and stoic. Talking takes a real toll.

The bus flashed past young shepherd boys and girls in traditional garb, pushing flocks of sheep to and fro. Their ancestors were probably shepherds when the angels sang at the first Christmas across the sea. In Bolivia, you just didn't leave the family business. Not much had changed in the way the rural people did things over the past two thousand years, except for the occasional set of Walkman earphones on the head of a teenage shepherd with his crook and traditional poncho.

I watched a father and son urging a flock of sheep down a dry streambed. My guess was they went for hours without saying a word. Yet their lives were as linked as a pair of shoes. They probably couldn't imagine a life without each other in it.

As a missionary I'd envied that in the men and boys I saw— that deep connection.

I envied it now. Dads teaching their sons always touched my heart.

I never had a lot of that. In fact, it must have been five years after my mission before I realized the reasons I'd given for going were mostly smoke. I had gone on a mission because my dad couldn't imagine me not going. And I went to win his respect.

I might as well have tried to please a sequoia tree.

My father was, by temperament, a military man. He'd commanded a bomber in World War II then brought all the lessons he learned about toughness home from the war with him. He saw everyone as either an ally or a threat. When he met people, he'd take their measure. Is this person a friend? If so, what can he do for me? If he's a foe, can I walk through him?

Dad would use his big voice to intimidate his foes, and he kept his allies in line with his laser wit. He often motivated people by embarrassing them and loved nothing more than to move great groups of people around—students, ward members, Lions Clubbers—by the force of his will and vision. He would have made a marvelous Bolivian general.

He seemed to me, then and now, to be a breed of prehistoric creature, wearing his skeleton on the outside to shield his inner parts. There was always one type of boy who took a shine to him as a teacher. They were usually boys with weak or absent fathers who were looking for discipline and direction in their lives. And Dad was happy to oblige. He helped dozens of them. I hear from them now and again. They remember my dad as a version of Noah, a strong-willed soul offering safety from the rising waters. But to me, he was more like King Noah, burning anyone at the stake who dared to stand up to him. Around our house, we three boys, Dave and Val and I, just tried to stay out of his way. He'd hoped for three stout-hearted men. Instead, he got a poet, a scholar, and a musician. We grew accustomed to the look of disappointment in his eyes. The Freud in me wonders if he didn't see us as rivals for my mother's love—rivals he couldn't destroy but had to endure.

He was an LDS bishop with an attitude, a music teacher who felt he needed to be double tough just to prove he wasn't soft. Ironically, he and I were probably more alike than different on the inside. But outside we were the lion and the lamb. I was too faint-hearted for my own good, and he was too forceful for his. And when I realized I could never win his approval, I turned to other figures to be my role models. Though I lacked the skill and nerve to be a star, I played baseball like it was a calling. I idolized Nellie Fox, the White Sox second baseman, and turned him into a dream dad.

Fox kept a wad of chewing tobacco in his cheek.

I imitated him with shredded brown licorice.

He wore number 2.

So did I.

His hair was receding. He had a widow's peak. With the dog clippers I trimmed my hair to match. My friends had no idea what I was up to. They just saw me as a freak.

As I aged, other substitute fathers came along. In 1965, the angry young folksinger inside me embraced Bob Dylan, though I had no idea then that he, too, was seeking a father. As a boy, Dylan visited the ailing folksinger Woody Guthrie in a New York hospital and began writing the same kind of political protest songs that made Guthrie famous.

Dylan didn't wear his hair in a widow's peak. He wore it in wild, curly locks—like his surrogate father, Woody Guthrie.

We were both two bewildered boys looking for some Tambourine Man to follow.

When writing poetry became my passion, I surrounded myself with a full stable of mentors. Most were flattered to have a disciple and rewarded me with compliments and kindness. One bearded old Spanish poet, Ángel González, almost filled the bill as a family patriarch. He looked and acted like a big Angora cat and wrote poetry as heavenly as his name.

Still, the magic in the relationships was always missing something. There was no tug in the blood, no genetic hum. In time, I would come to see even the religious leaders of my faith—men who could have helped me to understand myself—as simply versions of my father. They were men in suits who told me what to think and how to behave. They were like Dad, except they seemed even more distant and unknowable. The sound of their voices wafting down from the pulpit at General Conference reminded me of the sound of my father's voice at the top of the stairs. Their dire warnings chimed in my mind with my father's constant threats.

Feeling claustrophobic and constrained, I bolted from the Church soon after my mission and remained spiritually at large for the next twenty years. Then two events knocked me to the ground—one spiritually floored me and the other literally floored me.

Oddly enough, my father—bent and broken by bad health and despair—would be driven to his knees at about the same time I was. His military demeanor cracked and the crust around his hidden heart split to give a glimpse of the soft bread inside. The man who once fancied himself a more manly version of John Wayne began tearing up while watching old Grace Kelly movies. He even found the freedom of playfulness.

By then I was in my fifties, and his end-of-life softening—though very touching—had little effect on me. Holding his feet to the fire for how he'd treated me as a boy would have felt more like revenge than justice. And talking to him was tricky. My father had no stomach for revisiting old wounds, especially wounds he'd inflicted. What I saw as crippling and life changing in the past he regarded as yesterday's news.

He was tough on me, he once said, to toughen me up so I could deal with the world.

The ploy failed. I just retreated into myself.

And there was no going back.

Until the day he died, my dad never saw the difference between being tough and being strong. In the end, we were who we were. Our course had been run. Our relationship was forever set in lead. There was nothing to be said.

I never told him any of this.

As the bus neared the settlements outside of Oruro, I wondered how much of the Oruro from my mission would be left. For centuries the little outposts in the area had been ghost towns just waiting to happen. Booms and busts in mining were always at hand. As for Oruro itself, I wondered if the old bread factory where we held church would still be around. Could I find the old post office or the restaurant where we'd get T-bone steaks from Argentina?

I had a day to find out.

In La Paz I'd bought an ill-fitting leather hat that made me look like a wannabe Indiana Jones. I gave it to the first kid I saw in Oruro, prompting his mother to chirp, "But, sir, your head! You'll fry!"

In Oruro, 90 percent of the people were Indian and probably 98 percent of the men had a full head of black hair—even the eighty-year-olds. It would not be the last concerned remark I'd hear about my poor, bare-naked head.

My plan was to meet up with President Adrian Velasco, one of the city's stake presidents, then track down that old bakery and a few other landmarks from my mission.

I found President Velasco dressed in jeans at the church, working frantically to find rides for all the Saints who wanted to attend the temple dedication in Cochabamba. They longed to see President Hinckley. If it was true that "man was just a little lower than the angels," then for Bolivian Mormons the LDS apostles were pretty much at angel eye level. In one town, I recalled, we had to take down the portraits of the living apostles hanging on the church wall to keep members from praying to them. I suspect it went back to that business of everybody needing a patron. In the Catholic Church all the patron saints were dead. But in the Mormon Church they were alive and well and living in Utah. The LDS apostles were St. Francis and St. Christopher in flesh and blood.

As for President Velasco, we spoke for a few minutes about the wonders of the Spirit and the challenges of running a mortal organization. I saw the same authenticity in his eyes that I'd seen in Brother and Sister Gutierrez. I wondered if something noble in their shared ancestry made them that way. I know too much can be made of the notion of the "noble natives." But you can't deny what your experience tells you. And I kept seeing people who were lowly in the eyes of the world, but high and mighty in the eyes of God. It was a classic case of the last in the world being first in the Kingdom. Baptisms had come easy in Oruro in my day, and healing miracles were common. I'd loved the town and people for such reasons.

The little mining community of Oruro sat at the end of the Altiplano and also at the end of the known world. Pterodactyls could have flown by and not drawn a glance.

In the 1960s there was no television and no long-distance phone service. Mail was hit and miss. I once got a package for Christmas that had been sent to me the previous Christmas. We communicated with the outside world by telegram.

JOHNSTON TO ORURO (STOP)
RHODES BP (STOP)
SITERUD DL (STOP)

But if life in Bolivia was physically draining, it was also spiritually intoxicating. And being back was like a spiritual transfusion. But what made my heart really quicken—and made my acid reflux kick in—was finding the little bakery where we'd held church. The place was still hard at work pumping out dinner rolls. The "upper room," where we held our meetings, was still there as well. On fast Sunday the smell of fresh bread made fasting agonizing, though we always had great-tasting sacrament bread.

I knocked on the door, and a man in his thirties answered. I recognized him as the owner's little boy who, thirty years before, was always underfoot.

We stared at each other, like Stanley and Dr. Livingston.

"I used to be a Mormon missionary here," I said. "We held church above your bakery."

He eyed me, held up a finger, then ran off into the house. He returned with a wrinkled photograph—a photo of my companion Elder Jim Rhodes and me with other elders. I touched my face in the photo.

"That's me," I said.

He looked at the photo, looked at my poor naked head and my expanding belly, then he looked back at the photo.

"No," he said, wagging his index finger back and forth.

"Yes," I said. "It's me. Look."

We both looked down at the photo again. I was wearing the tie another missionary had given me when he left for home. I was also wearing a sappy grin. I looked as innocent and wide-eyed as the people I presumed to teach. I was so thin I could have walked through a harp.

That young elder in the photograph had no idea how much pain and frustration he was going to cause himself—and others—in life. He had no notion at all of the many detours and missteps that awaited him. He thought the world was his oyster and he was the pearl of great price at the center of it.

The kid in the picture was a photo portrait of "clueless."

I stared at the photo. So many mission memories had come flooding back over the past couple of days that I felt I was actually back on my mission. For a moment I became—again—that beaming elder in the photograph. I was once again a twenty-year-old elder searching for lost souls while trying to find his own. It was again 1969 and I was feeling tickled to the bone. I was about to meet a modern-day Malachi—a man who, over time, would become quite likely the greatest man I would ever know.

CHAPTER THREE:

Follow Me, Boys: Gordon B. Hinckley, Spring 1969

BEFORE 1969, NOBODY HAD HEARD of Butch Cassidy and the Sundance Kid. But in the movie that would make them legends, the two bandits go to Bolivia. When they climb from the train they're greeted by some wandering llamas, a few rattle-trap shacks, and a million miles of wasteland.

"All Bolivia can't look like this," Butch says.

"How do you know?" says Sundance. "This might be the garden spot of the whole country. People may travel hundreds of miles just to get to this spot where we're standing now."

But, as usual, Sundance was wrong. The garden spot of Bolivia then—and now—was Cochabamba, a lush little valley town six hours from La Paz. We elders called it "The Land of Milk and Honey," because that's what it was. "Coach" was one city where you could drink fresh milk and eat fresh honey every day at breakfast. It was also flat. You could ride bicycles there. And it was low enough so that even Americans could run and not be weary, walk and not faint.

Elder Tom Coleman, my companion, and I were working in Sucre, the country's former capital, when we got a telegram telling us of a mission conference in Cochabamba with the dynamic young apostle Gordon B. Hinckley.

For us, it felt like winning a trip to Honolulu.

In the states, 1969 was the year of the moon landing, Woodstock, and the Miracle Mets making it to the World Series. But for missionaries in Bolivia, the social event of the season would be Elder Hinckley's visit. He had been put in charge of Latin America in 1968 and—true to form—had immediately set out to see things firsthand. There were only eight missions in South America at the time, but within months he would have several others up and running. And Bolivia would be his first stop on a whirlwind trip south. He would also be dropping by Peru, Chile, Argentina, Ecuador, Colombia, and Venezuela to pay his respects. It was a platoon leader's approach to leadership. Elder Hinckley wasn't one to say "Go and do." He preferred "Follow me, boys!"

We didn't know about his other mission visits, of course. We just knew he was coming to Bolivia to meet with us. And while I scribbled excited notes in my journal about that visit, Elder Hinckley was jotting in his own journal as well. On April 11, 1969, he wrote about landing in La Paz:

"You feel all right at first," he wrote, "but if you start to move around too quickly, you begin to feel a little lightheaded."[1]

And his first impression of the people was the first impression most of us had:

"They are living for the most part in conditions bordering on the verge of desperation. Their poverty is so terrible . . . My heart ached. They deserve better."[2]

While Elder Hinckley made his way to Cochabamba from La Paz, Elder Coleman and I were making our way there from Sucre. Getting to Cochabamba meant a ten-hour bus ride on unpaved canyon roads filled with hairpin turns. But we were game. America's youth never fretted over their own mortality. And every twenty-four hours in Bolivia brought one kind of challenge or another.

I threw up twice on the way. If you didn't keep your eyes focused on the road ahead, you soon felt you were riding on a Tilt-a-Whirl.

We arrived on April 16, rattled and dusty. We had breaded veal for dinner then joked and joshed with the other elders and sisters, sharing a tangy mix of horror and faith-promoting stories from our various cities. The following day we planned to play touch football, do some sightseeing, and, in the evening, have a steak banquet followed by remarks from Elder Hinckley.

We felt as giddy as soldiers on leave.

Elder Hinckley had come into the country early to meet with the mission president and the elders around La Paz. So he had the lay of the land—and our mission—by the time he spoke to us.

Looking back now, he was the same Gordon B. Hinckley I would meet in Cochabamba thirty years later at the temple dedication. I even went back and read his General Conference address from October 1969 where he talked about his trip to visit us. He sounds, in that talk, as he always sounds—his sentences short and strong. His English bold and punchy, clear and transparent. It was the kind of speech that left no doubt the speaker had no doubts. To crib a thought from Randall Jarrell, when Pres. Hinckley spoke, even the dogs and cats could understand him.

"I do not want to boast," he told the Saints at General Conference that fall. "Heaven knows we have problems among us. We are far from perfection. And yet I have seen so much of good that my faith constantly strengthens . . . I believe in our youth. I believe in their goodness and decency. I believe in their virtue. I have interviewed thousands of them on a personal basis. Yes, there are some who have succumbed to evil, but they are a minority."

Consistency and steadiness were two qualities that during my wandering days I would associate with living in a rut. But with the years I have come to recognize Gordon B. Hinckley's life not as a life in a rut, but as a life of ritual. He never found life boring because the Spirit kept everything around him new—the way it keeps a scripture fresh after a hundred readings. He didn't need novelty to feel alive. The Holy Ghost kept him stimulated enough, thank you. And being true to himself and his faith—being grounded so the Spirit could work its electrical wonders—would become a Hinckley hallmark.

At the mission conference in 1969 he spoke to us, I recall, about "Ten Things to Take Home from Your Missions." From time to time in his talk he'd drop the Spanish word *maravilloso*—marvelous—always to a smattering of chuckles. Decades later, when I'd hear him caress the word *marvelous* in his conference talks, I'd wonder if he developed an affection for the word while in Bolivia.

In my typical fashion, I didn't take notes that night, and I remember no specifics from his talk. The fact I listed everything I ate at the conference and almost nothing I heard says all you need to know about me. But I do remember the feelings of lightness and laughter in the banquet room. And I remember a man standing before us who was earnest and focused. Like a sea captain, his demeanor seemed to say, "Steady as she goes."

Years later, I would come to see two sacred LDS symbols as emblems of the Hinckley way—the square and the compass. They were tools for making sure things got done right.

As for the square, I can still hear Elder Hinckley speaking plainly to our corps of missionaries, moving his right hand up and down like a man with a hammer. He would speak that same way thirty years later at the temple dedication. He measured twice and cut once. He squared every corner. Like the Savior, he was a builder. He loved to build things—buildings, programs, testimonies, character. He personally designed the Monticello temple where, at the dedication, journalists found him inspecting the miter joints in the doorways. He liked things to be plumbed and squared.

But along with the square, he was also the compass—or better, he was the metal spike in the middle that held firm while others whirled about. You always knew where to find him. He was in the center of things. He was as sturdy as a landmark and as helpful as a lighthouse.

And his visit to Bolivia was as spiritually refreshing for the elders and sisters as the rains called down by Elijah.

The day after the banquet, we missionaries said our good-byes and headed back to our towns to hit the streets, pumped full of zeal.

Elder Coleman drank a full quart of fresh milk before boarding the bus. He said he wanted to remember the flavor. He remembered it over and over. He threw it up all the way home.

I spent the ten hours on the road holding some woman's baby goat.

The day after the conference, on April 18, 1969, Elder Hinckley would again write about us in his personal journal:

"This is one of the amazing and wonderful things of the Church," he wrote, "to see the young people, who live under difficult circumstances and who have come out of such comfortable homes, express such tremendous love for the land and the people with which they labor."[3]

He was writing about us.

For, to tell the truth, Bolivia really hadn't changed much since the days of Butch and Sundance. In 1969 it was still a rough-and-tumble country. Tin was still king and the most impressive exports from Bolivia came off a loom or were carved from wood. Superstition was viewed as fact and facts were viewed with suspicion. Reality was what you voted it to be.

"Have you personally met Batman?" an old fellow once asked me.

You didn't dare tease the members with tall tales. They took you literally.

Butch and Sundance had left the Wild West of America for a fresh country. But many of those Wild West types were also down in Bolivia waiting for them. Most of them were still there in 1969—the big land owner, the military hardnose, the schoolmarm, the parish priest. All of them with faces from central casting.

In the weeks following Cochabamba, a new spirit began to buoy me along. In one letter home, I recall, I predicted a Bolivia temple would be built.

Today, the remark smacks more of a young elder trying to say important things to his parents than any gift of foresight. But the thought was typical of South Andes elders in the 1960s. We were knights on a spiritual crusade.

I know it has become fashionable to view LDS elders as wide-eyed innocents who speak in voices that sound like characters from an animated movie. And we were, indeed, young and impulsive—me more than most.

But we weren't afraid to be earnest. We loved our families and said so through tears. We saw ourselves as part of something large. We didn't trade in the winking irony that has become the mainstay of modern American movies and musicals.

Irony is easy.

Earnestness is hard.

And though we were lighthearted, we were filled with gravity.

Looking back, I view us as bumblebees or maybe one of those B-24s that my father flew. We carried so much weight there was no reason we should have been able to fly. We were weighed down with responsibilities, illnesses, fears, longings, and confusion. With such burdens there was no way to soar.

But we did.

We were weighted and buoyant.

We were airborne metal.

Arrowheads.

Bullets.

One week after our watershed conference, the president of Bolivia, René Barrientos, visited Cochabamba in his helicopter. The helicopter crashed, killing the president and his pilot. As a show of respect, the government declared that all businesses and government offices would be shut down for three days of mandatory mourning. Hardship followed as people scrambled for food and services. Even the elders were forced to scrimp.

Looking back at those three days of mourning, however, I'm convinced the sadness we missionaries felt in Cochabamba at saying farewell to Elder Hinckley was greater than what Bolivians felt for their departed president.

Like Shakespeare's King Henry, Elder Hinckley had come down into the trenches to lift us up. He'd put himself out there. He'd searched us out to give us "a little touch of Harry in the night."

And we loved him dearly for it.

That was in 1969.

Thirty years later—the year 2000—the country actually did have a new temple. And I was on my way to Cochabamba to write the first draft of its history.

As my bus huffed and growled into Cochabamba, just as it had three decades earlier, I didn't know it yet, but at the dedication I'd be singled out to carry the torch for the hundreds of elders and sisters who had left their hearts buried in Bolivian soil. I'd be given a privilege that dwarfed everything I'd done before.

My moment of truth had come.

CHAPTER FOUR:
A Millennium Every Morning

As I CHUGGED THROUGH THE outskirts of Cochabamba en route to the bus station, I noticed a stranger in town. On a high hill stood a giant statue of Christ—El Cristo de la Concordia. It hadn't been there in 1969.

His arms were spread in a way so you couldn't tell if he was beckoning the world or hanging on an invisible cross. It looked like the Christus on Sugarloaf above Rio de Janeiro in Brazil. But I soon learned the Cochabamba Christus was taller. The Brazilian version was thirty-three meters—one meter for each year in the life of Jesus. Cochabamba's was thirty-three and a half meters. The Bolivians figured Jesus lived just beyond thirty-three years. Bolivia loved to "one up" Brazil.

I vowed to visit the statue later in the day.

From the bus station, a cab shuttled me to the Hotel Diplomat where many Americans had set up camp. The place had a history. The first LDS service in Bolivia was held in Cochabamba, in a home near where the Diplomat stood.

I was road worn, and my annoying acid reflux was flaring again.

I went to my room to rest for an hour or two.

As I sifted through the contents of my luggage, I saw the column I'd written about my going to the temple dedication in Cochabamba that appeared in the paper a week earlier. I plopped down on the bed and read through it again, hoping to learn ways I could have made it better.

Writing a newspaper column was like working in a MASH unit. You did everything on the fly and made do with what was around.

* * *

The Deseret News, April 22, 2000, C1

In 1969, an LDS apostle visited Bolivia for the first time. He gathered us for a big conference in Cochabamba . . . His name was Gordon B. Hinckley.

Last week I found the letter I wrote to my parents about his visit. It was dated April 23, 1969: "Wednesday afternoon all the elders got together in a meeting where we exchanged ideas and had some talks," I wrote. "That night Elder Hinckley flew in from La Paz. He is sure a lot older than he used to be, but he still has a good sense of humor."

* * *

That was more than thirty years earlier. And not only was President Hinckley still alive, he was running laps around the rest of us. I remembered the day he told an aging jogger at the *Deseret News* that he didn't jog himself. He just spoke at the funerals of his friends who did. He would later speak at the man's funeral.

I read on:

* * *

As I go through the letters I sent home, I feel both amused and annoyed at the young man who wrote them.

I also feel affection for him. He knew so little and was glib about so much. And he seemed to have mastered only two adjectives: "sharp" and "tough." ("Say hello to Elaine. She sure is tough." Or: "We have a really sharp district and are teaching some sharp investigators.")

Hardly the work of a budding writer.

He was a kid who would fast for forty-eight hours over the health of a baby, then break his fast by eating ten chocolate bars.

He was a kid who got just as excited over being named quarterback for the zone football team as when he found a golden family.

Still, I admired him. He was willing to fling himself into the arms of Providence with no thought about his personal health and safety.

When a group of student protesters chased him through the streets of Sucre, the event got only a footnote in his journal.

When dysentery hit him so hard he couldn't lift his head, he had no doubt he'd be fine.

* * *

I remembered that moment well. I'd been so sick I could hardly speak, but I insisted on attending a branch picnic. We took a bus to the countryside. After lunch, I lost control of everything. Elder Hamaker led me into a nearby meadow, found a deep hole, and put me in it. I shed my clothes, gave them to him, and curled up like a fetus.

Hamaker took my clothes to the river to wash them. While he was beating them against the rocks and laying them on the grass to dry, as he'd seen Bolivians do, a group of young women left the picnic and started walking through the meadow. Hamaker raced back and yelled at them to go away. They thought it was a game. They surrounded the two of us (I was still down in the hole, naked). In a panic, Hamaker began winging dirt clods at them. He said later he feared the flying clods had driven at least three of them from the Church.

After my clothes dried in the sun, I got dressed and Hamaker led me back to the camp. The other elders gave me a blessing, and I could feel the illness lift from me like a wet sheet.

So it was in Bolivia in 1969.

Miracles were more common than colds.

Earlier, I mentioned that when the current missionaries I met on my trip to the dedication asked what Bolivia was like in the 1960s, I'd say, "Like this." The comment was, yes, a kind of backhand slap at Bolivian leaders for not doing more to make a better nation and take care of the people. But the thought was also a backhanded compliment.

In spiritual matters, the country still hadn't lost its soul. Bolivia was still a playground for the spiritual. People believed. They trusted. They had the same connection to spiritual matters that their ancestors had.

They were people of faith.

I could remember Elder Rhodes blessing a dying baby. The next day the doctor accused the mother of switching babies and bringing in a healthy one. I'd heard stories of elders restoring people's hearing, clearing up their eye problems.

Everything we said and did seemed larger than life. In our minds and hearts we felt we were in a fierce battle with the darker side of creation. We were warriors. At times we even felt invincible. We didn't handle snakes, but we did other things just as foolhardy. We'd eat food from street vendors whose cooking kettles were little more than petri dishes for cultivating hepatitis. We were daring. If we could get twenty minutes with the Catholic archbishop, we knew he'd be Mormon when we left. And if we could just run for mayor, we'd make the little towns where we served more efficient, just, and sanitary.

They were heady times.

Every new day felt like we were being reborn or—like Adam— being dropped down in the middle of creation for the first time.

Bolivia may have been at the bottom of the food chain in the Kingdom of the World. But it was a magic kingdom, a place where people bore witness to personal visions and prophetic dreams as often as they discussed the soccer scores.

As in the celebrated novels of Latin American authors, the supernatural and natural worlds blended seamlessly in our mission. And when I went back thirty years later for the dedication, it was still the same. If a member told you her grandmother had paid her a visit, you never knew if the woman had come from another town or another world. Daily life pushed so-called reality into soft focus and brought the inner workings of the heart into high relief.

Bolivia was a land of marvels.

It wasn't just a repository of superstition—a castle in the air.

In spiritual matters, it was a great fortress for the spirit, with watchtowers in the clouds and its foundation firmly in the ground.

Bolivia wasn't Neverland. It was real, palpable, and pulsating. It wasn't a land created by an author filled with a fanciful imagination. You didn't have to slip through a looking glass or a wardrobe to get there.

You just had to get on a plane.

I remembered reading an interview with the Colombian writer Gabriel García Márquez. He said when he first began to write about the magical, mystical, mythical world his grandmother inhabited, his descriptions didn't live on the page. Then he realized, to bring them alive, he had to believe them.

Belief is the heat that turns dry kindling into flame.

Belief ignites the world.

And all of Bolivia burned with belief.

Thinking such thoughts in my Cochabamba hotel room, I felt again the surge of spiritual adrenaline I'd often felt in 1969.

I went back to reading the newspaper column I'd written:

* * *

There is a reason that leaders like Joan of Arc, Joseph Smith, and Mohammed were so young when they took on their tasks. If they'd been much older, they would have been old enough to know they were being asked to do the impossible.

They would have frozen up.

Just reading some of the harrowing events in my letters made me feel a bit frosty myself.

Eventually, I found the first letter I'd written home from Bolivia. It was dated June 9, 1968.

"One man here even spends the night sleeping on the ice-cold dirt floor of the church to guard the new piano," I wrote. "That's what I call faith. People up there don't realize how much one of these people would give just to see a temple, let alone go through one."

* * *

Before I'd headed south for the dedication, someone told me President Hinckley had seen that column, and it had made him smile—especially the part about him being "old" in 1969. Perhaps the column was one reason he would soon call my name.

I cleaned up, ate at the hotel, then set out to rediscover the town. Cochabamba was famous for its open-air markets, but I didn't stop and shop. I wanted to soak in the sights and sounds. During the silver boom, Coach served as the breadbasket for the rest of the nation. And farms were still the norm in the landscape. Tourist books sometimes claimed that Cochabamba had the most livable climate in the world. According to local lore, "The swallows never migrated from Cochabamba."

But the place wasn't all daffodils and daisies. The many streams flowing from the hills onto the plain were sometimes chocked with cholera. And the town was notorious for producing—and drinking—whole reservoirs of Bolivian home-brew liquor called "chicha."

In 1987, Henri Nouwen, the Christian moralist, published a book called *Gracias!* about the time he spent in Cochabamba.

"Cochabamba is, indeed, the garden city of Bolivia," he writes. "Staying at one of the most lovely towns of Latin America, I am reminded that violence, oppression, persecution, torture, and indescribable human misery are all around . . . Latin America: impressive wealth and degrading poverty, splendid flowers and dusty broken roads, loving people and cruel torturers, smiling children and soldiers who kill."[4]

Even now, at the time of the temple dedication, there'd been concerns that violent protests over local water rights would undermine the temple open house. Wary LDS authorities kept an eye out as they conducted the tours. The blustery dustups between the government and its citizens were stark.

Bolivia was still a powder keg, as it had been when Nouwen was there in the eighties and when I was there in the sixties. The revolutionary icon Che Guevara had been killed in Bolivia in my day. Sadly, in 1989, two Mormon elders would meet the same fate.

In short, Bolivia could be as lovely and as deadly as a jaguar. It could be both the "healing stick" of Moses and the fiery serpent.

I made my way to Cochabamba's main plaza, *El Catorce de Septiembre* (September 14). There I hailed a cab and had the driver spirit me to the temple grounds.

The open houses were still going on, so I followed my nose around the grounds for a spell to see what I could turn up. The temple, designed by a Bolivian architect, was thick and square, as if made from the great stone blocks that went into the ancient fortress Machu Picchu in Peru. The homes around the grounds weren't at all grand. In fact, most were tumble-down cottages with leaky roofs and windows. Unlike other places, the poorest of the poor lived next to the temple grounds in Cochabamba. I liked that. I thought of Alma's famous sermon to the destitute who'd been kicked out of their churches. He, too, I think, would have enjoyed the sight of these tiny bungalows basking in the glow of Moroni.

I worked my way around to the back of the grounds and climbed the hill. I could see both the Angel Moroni and the Christus. The sight made me wish the Church had more poets to capture such sights. In my mind, the Church had lost its best poet just a couple of months before. I would think of him a dozen times as I worked my way toward the Cochabamba temple. The name Agricol Lozano and the word *temple* were almost a spiritual rhyme. He'd been a longtime temple president in Mexico City. Beyond the Mexican border his name seldom surfaced. But in the Mexico City wards and stakes he had been as legendary as Montezuma.

I'd met him while looking for LDS Spanish poetry to translate. He spent so much time at the temple, I had to eventually phone him there. He was a short man, but sturdy and determined. The locals called him "President Panzer," after the Wehrmacht tank. ("I have a lot of nicknames," he told me.)

He'd been a mission president, a temple president, and a teacher who once ignored a state order to stop teaching religion in the public schools. The government put him under house arrest but had to release him when his students ringed his house and wouldn't leave.

And when the man sat down to write poetry, he wrote like no other Mormon I knew.

"I write in gulps," he told me.

And that was how you had to read it—gasping for air. He once wrote a poem about a temple sealing that spoke of "the fire of the holy spirit in the moist kiss at the altar."

I called President Lozano in Mexico and asked him to send me some of his poems. He sent me a half dozen. Each one cascaded down the page, like this snippet from "Yo soy" ("I Am"). I think it is a poem that shows the grandeur of God filling the "temple of nature."

The mediocre translation is mine.

Like the mountains,
I push up—and out;
Reliable, like the winter,
I send never-ending snows
To ride the ridges, slopes, and cliffs.
I give my word with honor and I endure.
Like the mountains,
I gather a thousand patterns
In my tattered clothes:
Groves,
Wings,
Alpine forests
The nests of condors.
That is what I am.
Or better,
What I would become.

I count Agricol Lozano among Mormon visionaries. He showed me a new brand of Mormon. As President Hinckley once said of Elder Neal A. Maxwell, I don't know if we'll see his likes again.

I finished my outing by walking in a great circle around the Cochabamba temple, not unlike a Muslim on a pilgrimage. As I moved away from the crowd, I could see the Angel Moroni on top more clearly. He seemed tipped to the side and tilted upward, as if he'd been buffeted by a stiff wind. Then I realized he was pointing his trumpet at the Christus on the hill.

Each morning the sun would rise, ignite the gleaming white Christ, and—seconds later—bring Moroni and his trumpet to life with a burst of light.

Every morning in Cochabamba was a dress rehearsal for the Second Coming.

It was the Millennium, every morning.

I found my cab driver and told him to take me to the Christus.

CHAPTER FIVE:
A Model Child

THE CLIMB UP THE SPIRAL path to the statue had my acid reflux going, but I finally reached the top and looked back over the city toward the temple. It stood out in the city lights below like a white-hot coal.

I took a seat near the edge on the cement wall. I was the only one there.

I turned and looked up at the Christus.

Back in the stake center in Brigham City, a framed print of Christ descending amid clouds and blaring trumpets filled part of a wall. I'd often sit in an overstuffed chair there and ponder it. I simply could not conceive of a world without Jesus in it. I pride myself on my imagination and my ability to play "what if," but try as I might, I could not fathom existence without Him. And I suspected His detractors couldn't either. He was as much a part of the world as Mount Everest.

Over the years I had worshipped Him, denied Him, dismissed Him as a myth, and thought He was too complicated to understand. I once wrote a country song about Him, about how He followed me around. "I left his footsteps long ago," the song went, "but he won't step out of mine."

But I could never pretend He didn't exist.

At different times I'd been drawn to different aspects of his life. The Savior had more facets than a solitaire diamond. He was a Master Creator and Master Counselor, the wisest of patriarchs and a brilliant poet. But my simple faith always returned, like a lost boy, to the simplest Jesus of all: Jesus the Christ Child.

The most revered saint in the Catholic Church was St. Thérèse of Lisieux—Thérèse of the Child Jesus. The book she left behind, *The Story of a Soul,* is filled with innocence and purity. Her path to God, she said, was a "little way." She was determined to find heaven by doing small, childlike deeds on earth. Jesus the young child filled her heart. When she was tiny, she said, she'd see the Southern Cross made of stars in the night sky and thought Jesus had written her initial "T" there to please her.

Jesus the Christ Child would never dash such a sweet belief.

So little is known of the Savior's childhood that, over the centuries, folktales have surfaced to fill in the blanks. One of my favorites tells of angels bringing him toys made of gold. But Jesus ignores the toys, choosing instead to make little birds out of clay and bless them until they fly away.

From the time I was a boy myself, I'd felt that Latter-day Saints had a special appreciation for Jesus as a child. Mormons had a sweet tooth for the Spirit that led them to the Savior's basic innocence and simplicity. For me, some of the most touching moments in LDS meetings happened when adults sang one of the Primary songs as part of the service. Hearing grandmothers and grandfathers sing "Teach Me to Walk in the Light" or "I Am a Child of God" was always enough to bring tears to my eyes.

"Whosoever therefore shall humble himself as this little child," the Savior taught, "the same is greatest in the kingdom of heaven."[5]

Dozens of good lessons have been wrung from that thought. But the one I hold most dear would go something like this:

> Like children, we must not only be dependent on our Heavenly Father, we must recognize that dependence and follow him. Children know they would have nothing to eat, no place to sleep, and no protection without their parents. They are powerless. They don't kid themselves with illusions of "self-sufficiency." Children know we are all as vulnerable as butterflies.

That is the place our hearts must eventually reach—knowing

we are completely dependent on God for everything.

And since Jesus was the model of everything He preached, He, too, had the same type of heart, the heart of a dependent little child. I hear that childlike dependence in the Lord's Prayer. To my mind, it's a child's prayer, filled with the kind of submission only a child can muster. When pared down to its essence, the prayer says essentially the following:

Father,
You know what's best.
We only ask to be forgiven and nourished.
Lead us where you wish to take us.
Protect us as you take us there.

Perhaps my favorite moments in life were when listening to my wife, Carol, pray for me—pray for my health, my happiness. She'd talk in the same little song that children use when they pray.

She was, in every way, a child of God.

I took my cues from her.

When asked to speak at the baptism of a child, I let everything adult melt away. I talked of the Spirit being a piece of sunshine inside of us. It kept us warm. It helped us see things. It made us feel happy and safe.

And simplicity and sweetness are not just the hallmarks of Mormons but of all Christians. They are at the core of Christianity because they are at the core of Christ Himself.

And while sitting there on that hill in Cochabamba beneath the outstretched arms of the Christus, I remembered the day in 1997 when I'd interviewed Naomi Randall, the woman behind the words to "I Am a Child of God." I had asked how the words for the song had come to her.

"When I was young," she said, "my father began our family prayers with 'We, a few of Thy children, bow before Thee.' I never forgot that."

Naomi Randall—"Aunt Naomah," as everyone called her—passed away soon after we spoke. She had, at last, gone "to live with him someday."

I sometimes like to think of two masters of words and music, two Olympian talents—Franz Joseph Haydn and Robert Louis Stevenson.

Haydn gave us *The Creation* oratorio, a work of stunning power and passion. Stevenson penned *Treasure Island* and *Kidnapped,* two of the most gripping tales in the English language.

And yet, when their stunning gifts were joined in later years by some insightful soul, the song that emerged didn't rock the spheres and change the universe. It was a tender, touching song that every child can sing:

> *Thanks to our Father*
> *We will bring,*
> *For he gives us ev'rything.*
> *Father, mother, baby small,*
> *Heav'nly Father gives us all.*[6]

The Savior was King of Kings and Lord of Lords. He had a hundred wonderful names. But the most important was Child of God. He called God, His Father, Abba—Papa.

He acknowledged His total dependence on His Father. When people would steal from His Father or use their connections to His Father to feather their own nests, he'd let them know about it.

He loved His Father and was loyal to the last.

He was, in every way, a model child.

I stayed by the statue looking down at the city lights until there seemed to be no reason to stay longer. The next day I'd attend the dedication and begin compiling my *Church News* report. I wondered if President Velasco had arrived from Oruro. I wondered if any of my former mission mates would be in the crowd the next day.

Then I said a little prayer of thanks and slowly circled back down the hill. It was getting late, and the town was closing down. Despite its bustle, Cochabamba remained, at heart, a small town.

There were hot spots filled with vice, but nothing that threatened to flare into anything menacing.

At the base of the hill I looked back up at the resurrected Savior. My friend Randall Hall had once written a poem about the Christus in Brazil. He said the statue was white because Christ was filled with white light, like a prism. He held within Himself all the colors of the world. Light passed through Him and splashed down on Rio in a thousand hues. Christ was both the light, and colors, of the world.

I suspected that was also true in Cochabamba.

He was, indeed, a "Beautiful Savior."

I caught a cab back to the Diplomat hotel. As I went through my things in the room, I realized I had forgotten to pack a white handkerchief for the Hosanna Shout at the dedication the next day. I caught another cab and had the driver take me to a couple of clothing stores where I could buy one. But all the stores were closed. I would have to rely on God to bail me out.

It was fast becoming the theme of my trip.

CHAPTER SIX:
A Clean, Well-lighted Place

THERE WOULD BE FOUR SESSIONS scheduled for the dedication. I had a ticket to one of the first ones. I arrived early enough to soak up some of the atmosphere and drift in and out of conversations. A stake president told me he'd spent the morning cutting the grass at the stake center so it would be presentable for the prophet.

"Being a stake president in Bolivia is like being a bishop in the United States," he told me.

I thought of President Velasco trying to arrange rides for the Saints of Oruro well into the night.

One old gent posed so I could take his photo, his face staring at the temple in the stoic profile of an Inca warrior.

"*Hermano*," someone yelled, "not so serious. Smile!"

I took my place in line. Nobody seemed to mind having to wait. Waiting in line was never wasted time in Bolivia. People took the opportunity to make new friends and catch up on the news. When you're in line, there's no guilt for doing nothing. "I love to wait," my mother once said. She liked the guilt-free downtime.

At the door I struggled to put the plastic booties over my shoes. The more I tried, the less success I had. Finally, one sister came to my aid.

"Here," she said, "let me help."

She got down on her knees—in her nylon stockings—and slipped the booties over my shoes. Her gesture almost brought tears to my eyes. Did she know how close she'd come to washing my feet?

Inside, I took a seat next to a little grandmother. She had brought a purse filled with hankies for the Hosanna Shout, figuring nimrods like me would show up without a hanky. She kindly let me have one. When an usher came through with hankies for the forgetful, I took one and gave it to her as a trade.

The temple was built of "hand-hewn Comanche granite"— which felt rather appropriate. It had three sealing rooms, two ordinance rooms, and a baptistry. The Celestial Room was intimate and ornate with gold and white trim. The white carpet seemed to rise up to meet us.

The poet Wallace Stevens claimed there were "Thirteen Ways of Looking at a Blackbird." I decided there had to be a hundred ways of looking at a temple.

Over the years, in my newspaper column, I'd described temples as safety pins, keeping the fabric of heaven from tearing away from the earth like the lining of a coat.

When I taught kids about the temple I would sometimes put a picture of Jesus up high then put a temple between the ground and the picture. I told them temples were rest stops where we could catch our breath, plan our journey, and get some food for our long trip back to Jesus.

I'd written about temples and chapels as jewelry boxes—lovely cases filled with treasures seen and unseen.

I'd called them toolboxes—places where the implements for building eternal lives were stored.

I'd even compared them to those old "bread boxes" of the 1960s—filled with the Bread of Life. But nobody seemed to know what I was talking about.

I'd seen temples as versions of the human heart, complete with all its chambers and passageways. Moving into the inner rooms of the temple was an invitation to move deeper into ourselves. Dressed in white, we were like little temples ourselves, moving through a larger temple.

But it was my twin sisters-in-law—Jean and Janet—who led me to see the temple in a new way. They'd had so many disappointments in their lives that the family had lost count of their tribulations. But as they aged, they discovered the beauty and order of the temple. They loved the simple grace of it. Their faces seemed to gleam with a newfound peace. They became regulars.

It made me think of the Ernest Hemingway story "A Clean, Well-Lighted Place."

The story is set during the Spanish Civil War when Spain was in chaos. Each night a despairing old man makes his way to a small café, where he quietly sits and drinks. When someone asks a waiter why the man stays so late, the waiter says the place is clean, pleasant, and well lit.

Hemingway, who had little use for sentiment, sees the old man's quest for some sort of paradise as futile. And to make his point he rewrites the Lord's Prayer, inserting the word *nada*—Spanish for "nothing"—at every turn: "Our *nada* who art in *nada*, *nada* be thy name thy kingdom *nada* thy will be *nada* . . ."[7]

But a clean, well-lighted place—even a café in war-torn Spain—can indeed be a holy place. I'd witnessed as much in the small textile shop of the Gutierrez family in La Paz.

God was never absent.

He was always in the room.

When thieves robbed liquor stores, He was there.

He was there when children were abused and animals neglected.

He was there with the drunks and the desperados—always within earshot, hoping to hear a cry of the heart, ready to step in.

And in the Cochabamba temple—as in other temples—He was there in full force.

He wasn't "our *nada* who art in *nada*."

He was "Our Father who art in *todo*—in 'everything.'"

And wherever we found the courage to turn to Him, that place could become, for us, a place of worship—a clean, well-lighted place.

Many years afterward I would have the chance to speak at an LDS service in a women's prison and thought again of that day in Cochabamba.

The chapel at the prison had bright, white walls and simple benches. There was a single picture on the wall—a picture of Jesus. When the women came in, they were wearing white jumpsuits. It may have been as close to the temple as many of those women would get. The bishop said when you could get them away from their boyfriends and other bad influences, they often found themselves. When they went back to the world, however, many would lose their way.

In essence, he was telling me the women fared best in a "clean, well-lighted place."

We sat silently in the Celestial Room in Cochabamba. President Hinckley began scanning the assembly with his eyes. When he came to me, he smiled and moved on. Then, for some reason, he looked back at me in that friendly but riveting way of his.

He's going to ask me to do something, I thought. He's going to ask me to speak.

I pushed the thought from my mind.

What arrogance.

Relax.

But the "acid reflux" was again burning in my chest. Something out of the ordinary had happened. The room was different than it had been a few moments before.

Feeling foolish, I began to gather my thoughts and string them into remarks. You're behaving like a prima donna, I thought.

But in the middle of the dedication, the prophet rose and looked my way.

"Jerry Johnston of the *Deseret News*, a former Bolivian missionary, is here today," he said. "Jerry, come up here and show these people how much Spanish you can remember."

The eyes of the little grandmother beside me got as big as jumbo olives.

I stood at the microphone and gave a huff to relax. The loud sound startled everyone. I looked back at the prophet. He was wearing earphones, waiting for the translation of my choppy Spanish. I spoke for about three minutes. I talked of being a missionary in Bolivia and told about what I'd found on my current pilgrimage—the places where I'd seen the Kingdom of God at work. Most everything I said that day I've already said in this book.

President Hinckley listened intently. As I passed him on the way to my seat, he tapped my knee.

"Good job," he whispered.

I felt like the Little Drummer Boy being smiled upon by Baby Jesus.

As I sat down, warm tears filled my eyes. But then tears are always near the surface at a temple dedication. Among Mormons, tears are the calling card of the Spirit. Dervishes may dance, Evangelicals may raise their hands and voices, but Latter-day Saints quietly weep.

I thought of the times I'd seen President Hinckley lift his right hand to his mouth and give a little cough and realized he was on the verge of tears.

"My eyes are wet; my heart is full. The Spirit speaks today," a hymn declares.[8]

I figured it was no coincidence that the shortest Bible scripture was also one of the most powerful: "Jesus wept."[9]

Others stepped forward to address the gathering. I looked around the room and noticed several people had two hankies—one for the Hosanna Shout and one for their eyes. Perhaps the need to dry tears was why handkerchiefs originally became part of the Hosanna Shout.

Then it was the prophet's turn to speak. He spoke in a clear, firm voice—a voice filled with purpose. After each sentence, the interpreter would translate the words into Spanish, putting the same weight behind them.

The two of them were like lumberjacks with axes, felling a tree by trading blows. I'd never heard anything like it. The prophet—the carpenter—was driving his message home. I wondered if the Savior had delivered the Sermon on the Mount with the same forceful passion and power.

The *Church Almanac* reproduces part of President Hinckley's dedicatory prayer that day:

"We meet to dedicate this Thy holy house in Bolivia. How thankful we are for it. It is the fulfillment of our dreams, our hopes, our prayers, our faith."[10]

CHAPTER SEVEN:

The Best Is Yet to Come: Gordon B. Hinckley, Spring 2000

FOR CENTURIES, *The Pilgrim's Progress* was the most popular book in Christendom. Written in 1678 by John Bunyan, this allegorical story is about a quest. And the quick action fueled by startling illustrations—"graphics," we'd say today—made the book the world's first graphic novel and video game. You got in on page one, ran the madcap course, and emerged, at the end, to collect your pat on the back as a winner.

In the book, Christian, a young married man with a burden on his back, sets out for the Celestial City. He gets bogged down in the Slough of Despond and wastes too much time at the Vanity Fair. He's often distracted. Along the way he meets monsters and angels and other fellow travelers. But one character named Evangelist—the teacher—keeps showing up when Christian has lost his bearings, to help the young man get back on the path to the Celestial City.

In my life, the part of Evangelist has been played by President Gordon B. Hinckley.

He was always the constant in a sea of change.

And when he died in 2008, I don't know if his life flashed before his eyes, but it certainly flashed before mine.

I could see him, in my mind's eye, visiting Bolivia in 1969.

I saw him in those newsreel videos visiting Africa, where the Saints asked him to stand in the sun so his shadow would fall across them.

I saw him at various temple dedications, funerals, and dinners.

I also remembered the night when I was sent to seek him out on September 14, 2001, just seventy-two hours after the terrorists had leveled the Twin Towers. He was speaking with Larry King on the air from the KSL studios in Salt Lake City, and the newspaper sent me to get a quote or two from him when he finished.

He had told King, "Our hearts are all subdued . . . This is a time of national mourning and national resolve . . . We don't understand everything, but we do know our Father loves us."

I got the feeling King was taken aback by the prophet's optimism in such a dire time.

After the on-air interview, President Hinckley glimpsed Bruce Lindsay of KSL and me walking up. He smiled at us—his default reaction to most everything.

"Here, let me get my tin horn," he said, reaching for his hearing aid. It had been over a year since the temple dedication in Cochabamba, but where that day had been filled with joy, now the gravity of the moment was weighing heavy on him. Nevertheless, his faith shined through, as vibrant as ever. He looked tired and concerned, but his eyes remained clean and unclouded. For some reason, I thought of the paintings by Georgia O'Keeffe, where you can look through a pair of eye sockets deep into the blue heavens behind them. I don't want to overstate the experience, but I'd learned down the years that looking into the blue eyes of Gordon B. Hinckley could be like looking into the crystal pools in Yellowstone Park. The view went on forever. In my mind today, I often associate spiritual experience with the color China blue. Perhaps the eyes of President Hinckley play a part in that.

"President," I said, "last year in General Priesthood Meeting you counseled us to get out of debt and get our affairs in order. What counsel do you have today?"

His voice was as steady as the voice of an airline pilot.

"I think this may have fortified that counsel," he said. "I feel very strongly that we need to watch our temporal interests. It's always a good thing to have a reserve, get out of debt, be self-reliant, take care of your own needs, and live independently."

I pressed on.

"Some people will see apocalyptic visions in what's happened. What would you say to those people?"

He looked straight ahead with a fixed gaze as he weighed his thoughts, not like a man looking outward for answers, more like a man looking inward.

"Well, I don't know that I see apocalyptic visions," he said. Then he paused, as if being prompted through an unseen listening device.

"No," he said firmly. "But this is a terrible thing, the worst thing in the history of this nation.

"More serious than Pearl Harbor.

"More serious than the sinking of the *Titanic*.

"More serious than the worst air disaster that ever occurred.

"This was a thing unthinkable.

"But from it we can draw wisdom.

"From it we can draw strength.

"From it we can draw lessons.

"From it we can listen and get counsel concerning our lives and the need to live in a wholesome, good, conservative manner and keep this nation strong. The strength of the nation lies in the strength of its people. And we must do what we can as individuals to add to that strength and not subtract from it."

There was a finality to his last remark that seemed to say, that will do. He politely waited for me to speak again.

"Thank you," I said. He nodded, took his famous cane, and we all left together. Outside, I made long strides back toward the office. I would put several of his thoughts into a story, but I only included excerpts. That was a mistake. His comments to me about 9-11 were of one piece, made of whole cloth. You couldn't chop them into sound bites. Several readers wrote to complain about my editing of what he had said. They said I had deprived them of the full force of the prophet's words.

They were right.

I'd never make the mistake again.

The night President Hinckley died I was in the newsroom of the *Deseret News*. A photographer, August Miller, rushed in holding his cell phone. He said he'd just gotten a text message that the prophet had died. Six of us were there. We just stood and looked at each other, then everyone flew into action.

One person went to double-check the story. Another began laying out the preset pages of his life and various photographs on the floor like wallpaper samples.

I went to my desk and began writing a column.

For the next week, people devoured everything they could read and hear about the man. They couldn't stop reading. And I couldn't stop writing. I wrote one column about him right after his death, then a second a couple of days later. I started a third.

My first column was about his signature "prop," his famous cane. Today, it still sums up the feelings I hold close.

* * *

Deseret News, January 2008

> *Of all the photographs of President Gordon B. Hinckley, my favorite is the one where he is "knighting" President Henry B. Eyring with his cane. The gesture is playful, affectionate and—like so many things the man did—it holds a lesson.*
>
> *In the hands of President Hinckley, a cane was never a crutch.*
>
> *It was a tool.*
>
> *He took an emblem of weakness—a "walking stick"—and transformed it into an emblem of power.*
>
> *But then prophets have been doing that for eons.*
>
> *In the popular imagination, ancient prophets always carry a staff. They were always on the move—seeking people in the hills and valleys. Jesus sent his apostles out with "a staff only." Moses never left home without one. And when the apostles and prophets preached to the multitudes, they hoisted those staves to make themselves more visible, to broaden their reach.*
>
> *Who can forget President Hinckley entering the Conference Center, waving his cane above his head in greeting? He didn't*

walk with a cane. He used it to sweep cobwebs out of the corners. Like an orchestra conductor, he would lift it like a baton to bring people to attention and get them all on the same page.

Like a shepherd, he raised his staff to summon his flock—physically, mentally and spiritually.

Yet the biggest irony was—like the ancient ones before him—President Hinckley used his staff to bless, not injure. In the photo I mentioned, President Hinckley lifts his cane above the head of President Eyring, but there's no worry in his eyes. Let anyone else heft a club like that and the impulse would be find cover. But President Eyring simply smiles, his face that of a man awaiting a gift.

The photograph brings to mind the 23rd Psalm and the line, "Thy rod and thy staff, they comfort me."

That Psalm's beauty, Charles Spurgeon would point out, comes on the heels of Psalm 22 and the terrifying words that Christ would utter on the cross: "My God, my God, why hast thou forsaken me?"

They struck Jesus with a rod.

But he uses that rod to comfort others.

It's an odd notion, a staff comforting. Some Bible commentaries say the Psalm's "comforting staff" really represents leadership—somebody pointing the way. Matthew Henry quotes Leviticus, where shepherds would extend their staves and number their sheep as they scampered beneath the pole.

But I hold to the notion that a staff can actually bless and heel. The paradox seems very biblical.

A staff in the hands of a prophet is not a weapon. It's a lightning rod to call down the blessings of heaven. When he hoists a staff, a prophet points to a source of power beyond his own.

There are hundreds of photos of President Hinckley with his cane. And in each photo he turns a symbol of aging into a symbol of vitality and energy. No doubt he would say the source of his resiliency was not his own. It came from elsewhere.

There's a scripture that reads, "By faith Jacob, when he was dying, blessed both the sons of Joseph; and worshipped— leaning on his staff."

He may have leaned on his staff, but it was not a piece of wood that made Jacob upright and true. His support, too, came from elsewhere.

Prophets don't use their staves to help them relax. They use those staves to make sure we never do.

Anybody who's read the Bible will soon see that.

Anybody who reads the Bible, or has witnessed the miracle walking among us known as President Gordon B. Hinckley.

* * *

The last time I saw President Hinckley, my wife and I had been placed at his table for a company banquet. We spoke about hymns and heroes and *Huckleberry Finn*. I asked him if he'd ever had a mentor as a young apostle. He shook his head.

"He doesn't need a mentor," my wife said. "He is a mentor."

We chatted about music. He said his fondness for the song "Danny Boy" began when he'd first heard it on the docks in Ireland. A boy was singing the song for tips. We spoke about his trip to Africa. He said he'd love to mingle more with the people, but his "babysitters" wouldn't allow it. There was a wink in his voice whenever he spoke.

I asked him if he knew how many copies of his book *Standing for Something* had been sold. He didn't know. And I got the impression he didn't want to know.

We talked about growing up.

"Did you play sports in high school?" I asked.

"No," he said.

"What about theater?"

"No."

"What did you do in high school?" my wife asked.

He smiled.

"I went to school," he said.

He talked about an old textbook he'd found from his school days. How it was so dated it made him shake his head. The textbook had remained mired in the past. President Gordon B. Hinckley had not.

When he left, he took a moment and pointed to the big slice of chocolate cake next to Carol's plate. Then he flashed—again—a smile that could change the weather.

"Look," he said. "The best is yet to come!"

All of this, of course, would happen many years after the dedication of the Cochabamba temple. So to get back to the thread of my story, it is still the year 2000. We were in the Celestial Room for the temple dedication and the prophet was speaking to the Bolivian Saints.

He thanked them for all they had done.

He numbered their accomplishments.

He told them all the groundwork had been laid.

And now, he told them, it was time for them to begin.

CHAPTER EIGHT:
The Prodigal's Song

AFTER THE DEDICATION I STAYED around the grounds for a couple more hours, getting comments for my story. I took a photo of the Angel Moroni pointing his trumpet at the Christus on the hill for the *LDS Church Almanac*. Then I went looking for some salt-of-the-earth Saints. I chatted up a couple of sisters in the family history center. One shared a vivid, almost electric dream she'd had the night before. It had changed her life.

Dreams in Bolivia were as real as rain.

I got a bite to eat then caught the puddle-jumper flight back to La Paz.

That night, on television, I watched a minister rally his followers. An evangelical spirit had seized Bolivia and other Latin American countries, just as it had seized upper New York in Joseph Smith's day. Meanwhile, the LDS Church continued to grow and build from the bottom up and from the inside out, anchoring its congregations with new buildings and putting a system in place so the institution would flourish and the harvest of souls would flow smoothly.

I wondered if that was a reason the Mormons had survived the spiritual burnout in New York that followed the spiritual awakening of 1820. They knew how to organize.

The next day I caught a flight to Miami, where I checked into my hotel. I phoned my wife from my room and told her everything that had happened. She listened, speechless. I was still trying to process everything myself.

My Miami hotel was the one place where I'd decided I would pamper myself. It was top of the line with a first-rate restaurant and a classy bar. On my way to dinner I peeked into the bar.

Time was I would have strode in and let myself slowly sink into the soft music and easy shadows. Bars may be dark, but for drinkers, it's a plush darkness, a welcoming darkness. Bars are warm, relaxing sensory deprivation tanks.

Now, I stood five feet outside the door just looking in. It had taken me twenty years to move those five feet away. Yet it had been a five-foot journey with more switchbacks in it than a bus ride to Cochabamba. I ate dinner and returned to my room.

That night I began to knock together a column for the newspaper. I'd decided to leave me out of it completely. The idea would be for the writing to disappear and just leave the events and feelings on the page.

I wrote differently now than I had in my youth. Then, I'd seen myself as a budding wordsmith—a poet—so I crafted each sentence like a strip of inlaid wood to be placed on the face of a guitar. Now, with deadlines always looming and space to fill, I couldn't afford the luxury of too much craft. I couldn't even afford the luxury of writer's block. "When you feel writer's block coming on," a friend had told me, "Lower your standards and keep writing." My style now was to locate my natural, conversational voice and just ski on it down the page, trying to dodge the pitfalls as they arose like too many moguls. I wrote defensively, trying to avoid miscues.

Was I being too sentimental?

Too preachy?

Too stale?

Too obtuse?

Had I said that before?

Had someone else?

Once in a while I'd stop to puzzle out a symbol or metaphor that worked on more than one level, but usually the payoff wasn't worth the pain.

If I stayed limber and alert and could dodge enough mistakes, I usually finished at the bottom, still on my feet, with a piece that was not only understandable but bordered on competence. Then I'd go back to the top of the page and ski down again to smooth things out, then again, until I finished or simply got so tired of the thing that I abandoned it to the editors.

A columnist doesn't need to know what he's talking about to write a column. He just needs to sound like he knows. Subject matter can carry a column. But so can a likable voice. The way you said things became as important as what you had to say.

Of course, the biggest villain for columnists and other writers was distraction. And that was my bugaboo in Miami. My temple moment kept running on a loop through my mind, but nothing fresh emerged. Try as I might to become engaged, even the hotel art looked more interesting to me than what I was putting down on paper.

Finally, I put my notebook aside, lay down on the bed, and replayed the last few days. Then I began to replay—year by year—the twisting path that had gotten me to those last few days. Apart from family doings, being called to speak at the dedication of the temple had been the high point of my life.

How had it happened? What goose-necked river had I floated down to get there?

I looked back over the years and tried to mentally chart the course I'd followed. It had been an obstacle course, filled with real obstacles. Most of them put there by me.

Where Gordon B. Hinckley's life was an example of how to live, my life had been an example, too: an example of what not to do and how not to do it.

We like to say every life tells a story. Yet some researchers suggest each life is just a box full of random events. It's each individual who must thread them together to make a narrative, a story.

Every life doesn't tell a story.

But every person turns his life into a story.

In our heart of hearts, we are all Hemingways. We take the horrors and happy moments from our marriages and other rites of passage and string them together like a strand of pearls. And along the way we make ourselves the hero or the victim or the curious bystander of our own lives.

And in the strand of pearls that made up my life, there was a string of black pearls I often called "my wilderness years."

In hindsight, I was twice as lucky as Moses. He wandered in the wilderness for forty years. I only spent twenty years there. And though it would be comforting for me to cast myself as a noble seeker out in the desert, a heroic soul battling the darkness to find the light, I know better.

My life had more in common with bumbling Pinocchio.

Pinocchio left his home and father to knock about with a fox and cat—vagabonds who taught him that freedom was really just a knack for avoiding responsibility.

That happened to me, too.

Pinocchio was trapped by the shrewd puppet master, Stromboli. He indulged himself on Pleasure Island until he turned into a jackass and ended up grappling with a beast from the abyss.

That was me as well.

After my mission I began to drift. In my case, the "wrong friends" weren't boozers and ladykillers. They were cerebral types who prided themselves on seeing through ruses and shams. Many Mormons assume sin pulls a person away from the Church and a new way of thinking soon follows. But it's not always true. In my case, the thinking came first. Intellectual freedom was my cult, the life of the mind. Sinning came later.

I loved reading the poetry of John Berryman, the novels of Saul Bellow, and I loved taking them seriously, on their own, without filtering them through Mormon doctrine to be fumigated.

As one of my newfound friends would tell me, everybody's "mammon" is different. It's not always money. For some "serving mammon" meant seeking drugs or power or riches. For you, he told me, mammon was world literature. The life of the mind.

Still, I tried to keep one foot in the Kingdom of God and the other in the Kingdom of the World for as long as I could, but I knew something had to give. I no longer read the scriptures, paid tithing, or prayed. It was a matter of time before the candle of

Mormonism would begin to flicker out.

In 1973, weary of the patriarchal voices floating down from LDS pulpits and determined to chart my own course, I threw in with a Spanish professor at Utah State University for the school's Winter Quarter in Mexico Program. His students called him "El Profesor." I wanted to be a man of the world, and he was just the one who could make it happen. He made me the assistant director of the program.

There was a banquet being served by the world, and I'd been missing it for years. In their talks and testimonies, Mormons could make you believe a cruse of oil and a crust of bread was a feast. I didn't believe it. I saw a clueless sweetness to Mormon life—in the singsong way the children bore their testimonies, in the conventions and clichés. Their innocence was not bliss in my mind. It was just the symptom of an unlived life.

Instead, I would become a disciple of the God of Good Taste. Sophistication, not the celestial kingdom, would be my goal And I had handpicked my mentor—my father du jour—El Profesor. He would knock the hayseeds out of my hair and make me presentable in polite society. I took him on as my personal Henry Higgins, the genius who would remake me and give me a new life. I never stopped to ponder how badly the experiment in *Pygmalion* had ended.

El Profesor and I drew up a travel itinerary, concocted class schedules, arranged for homes where students could stay, and booked passage for fifteen students on a train from El Paso to Mexico City. We drove away from Logan, Utah, in a blizzard. By nightfall we were already rolling down the windows and looking at the flowers.

I was leaving the chilly Saints to find folks with more sizzle.

My mother, sensing I was poised to leap free of my upbringing, had slipped six packages of temple garments into my suitcase without telling me.

I would toss them all away.

As we rolled through New Mexico, the Prof entertained me with tales of love and lost innocence. I entertained him with my bad impersonations of Glen Yarbrough and Marty Robbins.

My twenty years as a stranger in a strange land had begun.

I was officially a fugitive from God.

We met up with our students in El Paso and boarded the train in Juarez, Mexico. The trip south was everything I'd hoped. Mexican railways remained a popular way to travel, and we'd booked first-class accommodations. I loved the fresh flowers and linen tablecloths that filled the dining car each morning. And in the club car at the rear, the tables had inlaid chessboards made from blocks of ash and mahogany.

The porters bustled about in their snappy white uniforms. Alluring young women would show up from time to time in the club car to read magazines and flirt. It was all so wonderfully decadent.

I took my first sip of champagne.

It was like riding the Orient Express in the 1940s.

The train clicked through little towns, slowing down just enough to keep from killing anyone. Ragamuffins begged at our windows, old women sold yellow corn tortillas that steamed in their baskets like freshly minted suns. The teeth of the old men—at least the teeth they had left—reminded me of yellow corn kernels.

The line between the "haves" and "have nots" was never so stark. And I was on the right side of the ledger. Life was unfair. But it didn't have to be unfair to me.

We arrived in Mexico City and settled in. El Profesor had set up classes in a little institute across the way from the deliciously bohemian *Zona Rosa*—the Pink Zone—where dandies and dilettantes talked politics, wrote bad poetry, and ate wonderful meals.

The Prof and I set up housekeeping in an apartment near the Angel of Independence monument, just up the street from the U.S. Embassy.

In the evenings we'd take a short walk to the Zona Rosa, where we'd sit at checkered tablecloths in small cafes and plan the next day's lessons. Then we'd head to some bistro for dinner, trading barbs and ironic asides along the way.

One evening, however, El Profesor did look me in the eye and, in surprisingly earnest tones, said, "If I had going for me what you've got, nothing would stop me."

I had no idea what he meant.

Stop him? Stop him from going where? Hadn't we arrived? Wasn't this paradise?

Years later, when I had a good friend die, I would remember his comment that night and realize the folly of a man-made paradise like the one I was living.

My friend died in France. During a rough patch in his life, he had moved to Paris to reinvent himself. He'd gotten a place to stay near the Seine and had begun pecking away at a novel. He'd e-mail me about its progress. Sometimes I'd smile, picturing him riding a bicycle with a long loaf of bread on his shoulder. He died suddenly and alone his first summer there while the French doctors were on vacation whooping it up on the Riviera. I think the sweltering Paris summer heat did him in. No one knows for sure. He was only in his fifties.

Here in America we mourned him deeply. They flew his ashes home, and a wake was held. But for me, his death also came with a quiet cautionary tale. It was this: Take care when you substitute your own notions of paradise for God's notions. You could end up dying while living out the script from some old Maurice Chevalier movie.

He was one of my newfound friends who had bolted from the Mormon flock. Many of them were now "hyphenated Mormons"—cultural-Mormons, historical-Mormons, jack-Mormons. And just as the Jews had been scattered and seeped into many cultures and countries, my new friends had alighted—like the puffs of a dandelion gone to seed—in a dozen different religions.

Some had found a comfortable "halfway house" with the Anglicans or Unitarians. Others had dug down and embraced Catholicism, which they saw as the root of everything that came later.

One became a Jew.

One became a Sikh.

They were all spiritual people on a quest.

I was, too; though I didn't know it at the time.

I saw myself as having outgrown the clothes of spirituality and was now trying on some spiffy new duds. And I liked the way the worldly air of Mexico City fit.

Religion was no longer part of my life.

I was a kid in a cosmopolitan candy shop.

And I was chowing down.

On weekends the Prof and I clubbed around town or went our separate ways to explore. During the week we behaved like tweedy professors, teaching Spanish to our band of acolytes at the Institute for Interpreters.

The Institute would be where my bourgeois ways would become set in stone. It was where, the first week of classes, I fell hopelessly in love—not with a student in our group, but with a young, blonde Italian who had eyes like a sad baby lion. She was taking English classes in the same place we were teaching Spanish. She was small and clever and seemed —to my new, man-of-the-world mind—to be a Madonna come down from some niche in a nearby church.

I asked her out to dinner.

She agreed to go.

As I boarded the bus for the suburbs where she lived, I recall El Profesor shouting after me, "Remember! White wine with fish, red wine with meat!"

It's about the only piece of advice he gave me that I still remember.

I arrived at the young woman's house and was greeted by her parents. Her mother was quiet, sweet, and domestic. Her father was a dashing, middle-aged man in Gucci shoes, a fancy watch, a tasteful pipe, and a theatrical Italian manner. I liked him right away. He read books on ESP and UFOs and had a Venetian's disdain for coarseness and the lower classes. The family's home was in Mexico, but in their food, customs, language, and music, they still lived in Italy.

That night the four of us chatted for a minute. Then the father suggested a restaurant called the William Tell—the Guillermo Tell—which I misheard as some "motel." He asked if I'd like to borrow his Mercedes. The wife and daughter were aghast. What had possessed him? His car was his pride and joy. He never lent it to anybody. But I think he saw in me an escape hatch for his daughter, who—like him—was trapped in the belly of a third-world country.

It turned out to be a grand night for romance—if you don't count the fact I shut her foot in the car door then later asked her to take a walk with me. She bravely hobbled along.

My life among the sophisticates had begun.

In the following weeks the daughter and I would see each other every day. We visited the town of Vera Cruz, where we behaved like a silly couple in a love song. We watched the young boys diving for coins in the marina, listened to the church bells, watched the homesick, lovesick sailors. Our every move was accompanied by the sound of marimbas. They chimed background music for us like a dozen velvet pianos.

Romance was out to do us in. We didn't stand a chance.

Back in Mexico City she and I visited open-air markets, kissed on the Pyramid of the Sun, and drove to Cuernavaca to dine among the peacocks and bougainvillea flowers.

I'd finish my hitch as assistant director, return to the States to work and save for three months, then return to marry her in a rollicking Italian wedding where uncles named Giorgio and Fernando kept stuffing money into my pockets.

We honeymooned in Acapulco.

We were walking, talking advertisements for "the good life."

Our marriage lasted seven years and produced one son.

The truth is our marriage was star-crossed from the very beginning. My Mormon parents, with their understated Western ways, made her feel numb and sullen. And, try as I might, I never mustered the drive for money and success that she felt a smart guy like me ought to show.

I got a master's degree in Spanish from the University of New Mexico, and in 1976 we moved back to Utah. I taught for a short spell then went to work as a sportswriter for the *Deseret News* in Salt Lake City. Like so many things in my life, landing that job seemed, to me, a lucky spin of the roulette wheel. But the truth was the odds had been rigged in my favor by someone who was keeping a watchful eye.

The *Deseret News* hired me because, to impress the editors, I dashed off a little piece about some hotshot kid at Roy High who could supposedly punt a football 100 yards.

The hotshot kid turned out to be Jim McMahon.

As for my wobbly marriage, my Italian wife followed me for as long as she could, then when I wasn't paying attention to her—which was often—she took her newfound American drive and ambition, traits which she had tried to ignite in me—and claimed them for herself.

She left and took my son, Ian, with her.

I would tell my friends that she took the car but left me the Spanish language. But such banter masked the fact I was devastated, sleeping on the bedroom floor next to the south wall because I knew another couple was close by the on the other side. I shuddered at being alone. I took to the nightlife. I began to roam. I dated every night—a Western swing dancer who could parallel park a pickup at fifty miles per hour, a ballerina who wore more ACE bandages than a linebacker. I got especially close to a Japanese journalist, a girl with blind parents and a femme fatale who charcoal-broiled my heart.

Yet I could never make things work. The women themselves were wonderful. But I was searching for a color in them I could never find—the same color I had tried to bleach out of myself: the rich, royal blue of spiritual kinship.

Still, through it all, I refused to abandon my pose as a man of taste, as a bohemian devil. But in reality I was little more than a second-rate drunk, a third-rate gambler, and a rather clumsy lady's man.

But I had booked my ticket to Pleasure Island, and I was going to ride it out.

My donkey tail and ears had already begun to grow, but I didn't care.

"Pride ruled my will," writes John Henry Newman in his hymn "Lead Kindly Light." "Remember not past years."

Oddly enough, I always kept within shouting distance of the Church. I didn't attend, but I worked hard to keep up connections with LDS friends. Dennis Baird and Ron Frandsen, a former bishop and future bishop, respectively, waited and watched with me as I stewed on my dunghill and wrestled with my demons. On darker days, my LDS colleagues at the paper would take me to lunch and help me wring my hands.

I also stayed close to a high school chum who had boosted my teenage self-esteem and station just by being seen with me.

His name was Randall Hall. I quoted a poem by him earlier. When not scoring touchdowns or acing the ACT, Randy's real interest was poetry. He was rather accomplished, and he took a shine to my dimly lit efforts. We began to hang out together in what we called "Dangling Conversations." We spent time in the hills and talked in metaphors as if they were our secret language.

After my divorce we'd meet for lunch in Salt Lake City and talk sports, literature, history—anything but religion. This went on for years. Looking back, I see now that must have been hard for him. He lived a Mormon life, donating his teaching skills, writing skills, and management skills to the building up of the Kingdom.

I think he could see I was closer to the Kingdom than I cared to admit, but he couldn't get me to cross the drawbridge.

I was also chatting up a psychiatrist at the time. The man told me I suffered from "separation anxiety," that leaving the Church had damaged my psyche, but my brain would heal.

It never did.

On top of that I was reading Camus and Sartre and had convinced myself I was battling "existential angst." I would just have to tough it out.

A folksinger said I had the blues and should sing out my pain.

A poker chum advised me to get drunk every chance I got.

Randy, however, knew me well enough to recognize my true illness. I was homesick—homesick for God, for my Heavenly Father.

Around my artsy pals I enjoyed mocking the sugary sweetness of Mormons, but in the pit of me I craved that very sweetness— the way a man awash in insulin needs a lump of sugar. People who mock the sweet nature of Mormons have never felt it. They take a few grains of sugar, rub them between their fingers, and say, "I can't taste a thing." They simply refuse to touch the sugar grains to their tongues.

I played the sarcastic wag in public, but in private I would get tears in my eyes while listening to Primary songs. I secretly still collected baseball cards and read comic books. I wasn't the steely sophisticate I pretended to be. I was a tin man, in search of a heart—a hidden heart that was already inside of me.

Randy, with his extended spiritual antenna, sensed as much. And, in the subtle yet honest comments of a lifetime buddy not wanting to curdle a friendship, he tried to tell me so. But he had to pick his spots. I was in no mood to hear the counsel of the Brethren. I imagined them sitting around at night, fretting over the fact that somebody, somewhere, was actually doing what they wanted to do. In my mind, the apostles were still my father, to the twelfth power.

Randy waited patiently as I floundered aimlessly and agonized beautifully. He was there when I began writing my newspaper column, when I won awards and when I got married again at age forty—married to a woman with four children who had grown up almost next door to me. And she was as Mormon to the core as Eliza R. Snow.

God was closing in.

Everyone could see it but me.

I'm not sure what makes up an "All-American Girl" these days, but I think a homecoming queen with a heart of gold has to still be in the running. That was Carol. She had been through the wringer, but instead of turning to psychiatry and booze—as I had—she had turned to the Lord.

Instead of becoming bitter, she'd grown more understanding.

I remember peeking into her high-school yearbook in the early years of our marriage and reading what her steady beau had written to her there.

"I'd like to thank you for the help and inspiration you have given me," he wrote. "You have always been behind me in everything I've done or tried to do. You have helped me live a better life. You have been a great example."

She was that same person in my life she'd been in his. Only now her colors were richer.

I read her boyfriend's words and thought, finders keepers.

My choice of Carol was like a flashing signal for Randy, my family, and my other friends. They could see I wanted to embrace my childhood faith again. I had a job at an LDS newspaper, I had a whole crew of new LDS friends, and now my wife was LDS. Everything in my life was LDS, except me.

My brother-in-law Wally took me aside.

"What's your relationship with the Church these days?" he asked.

"The Church and I do a little dance," I told him.

He scoffed.

"A dance?" he said. "Well, be careful. That wife of yours will have you cheek-to-cheek with the Church before you know what hit you."

Her father, Owen, wasn't worried. He'd taught animal husbandry to the 4-H kids at the high school, and he told me I was a calf with good bloodlines. He figured breeding would eventually win the day.

Her mother wasn't worried either. She'd fed me cookies when I was four years old and felt she got a reading of my soul at the time. She figured God had set his seal on my heart, and all of my worldly fussing about amounted to little more than theater.

Still, I was determined to play things out as a resolute outsider, the melancholy maverick.

After seven years, my marriage to Carol—with its split personality—began taking on water. Eventually I moved out. And while living in a little apartment across from the Cathedral of the Madeleine in Salt Lake City, one night I had a visionary daydream—just like my Bolivian comrades in Cochabamba were always having.

I saw myself walking the foothills above Brigham City when I came to a split in the trail. One path went up and over the top, the other drifted out and away into the valley. I don't know where that image came from. Perhaps I'd been reading Robert Frost's "The Road Not Taken."

What I did know was where each path would take me. The one that went down would lead me back to my former life—with its carousel relationships and quest for entertainment and other distractions. The other path, the one that rose over the hill, was my life with Carol. It was a troublesome climb, but it seemed to lead somewhere, to some land where we could live together. The upward path was a path with a future.

The next morning, a Sunday, I heard the Mormon Tabernacle Choir singing "There's a Place for Us" from *West Side Story* while I waited for the football game to come on. And where all the hymns had failed, that tune from a pop musical caused my heart to soften. I suspect now that most songs can serve as hymns, if you listen to them right.

I phoned Carol and told her I would attend church and give the gospel a go if she'd give me one last shot. If she'd take me back.

She didn't know what to say, so she said okay.

I moved back home the next week. I was under the same roof as Carol again, and under the wary gaze and watchful eyes of Erica, Helena, and Felicia, her three daughters. They kept their distance. They felt I was about as stable as heated mercury.

Returning to church, I was shocked at how many things had changed, or maybe how much I'd forgotten. I was singing hymns I'd never heard before and learning new names for the Young Women groups. I accepted a calling to serve in the nursery, and I helped with teaching where I could. But I still struggled to feel at home with it all. I couldn't quite get my balance. In short, I was a bumbling kid again learning to ice skate. My family and the ward members did their best to steady me. Friends held me upright as best they could. But I kept wobbling and slipping.

Then, out of nowhere, in what felt then—and still feels—like a bolt from the blue, the Lord sent me a tender mercy. A spiritual Olympian came onto the ice to help me learn how to skate. He glided to my side, extended his hand, and gave me—for the first time in twenty years—my sense of balance.

He taught me how to glide hand-in-hand with the Spirit.

He would become the most important friend I ever made.

CHAPTER NINE:
Eternity in an Hour: Neal A. Maxwell

IN 1980, ELDER NEAL A. MAXWELL was a member of the Quorum of the Seventy and the commissioner of Church Education. I was the book critic for the *Deseret News*. I wanted to do a series of stories on the favorite books of prominent people and called Elder Maxwell to ask if he'd contribute. He graciously agreed and mailed me his list.

"Jerry, I read intensively but sporadically," he wrote in his letter, "so that new books would replace the last two or three on my list, whereas the scriptures, for instance, have a deep and persistent value for me."

Some of his choices, like the scriptures, were naturals. "There is never any question of being disappointed when one ponders these pages," he wrote.

Mere Christianity, by C. S. Lewis, was on his list, along with *Democracy in America*, by Alexis de Tocqueville ("increasingly relevant"), and Elizabeth Longford's *Wellington: The Years of the Sword* ("excellent").

But one book caught my eye—the little gem, *A Gift from the Sea*, by Anne Morrow Lindbergh. He praised the book's "therapeutic perspectives in the midst of a busy and pressing world."

Generally considered a woman's book, *A Gift from the Sea* became a prototype for most of the slender volumes of self-help advice that followed. Lindbergh wrote about walking along the beach, where she picks up various shells. Each shell has a lesson to teach—how to be alone, how to dig deeper, and other insights.

The reason I flashed on its choice by Elder Maxwell was I often kept copies of the book around to give as gifts, though I seldom mentioned it when discussing literature with my academic friends. It was a guilty pleasure. I was, as I said earlier, still a disciple of the God of Good Taste. And lofty little tomes of spiritual awakening didn't qualify.

But Elder Maxwell was an academic and knew literature better than I did. And he had put the book out there for all to see, without a drop of self-consciousness or shame. He didn't worry about what others thought. He owned up to the things of his heart.

I had to admire that.

And I admired a mind that could be as hard and reflective as agate, yet still embrace tenderness and sentiment—even popular taste, froth and all.

I wanted to learn how to do that.

I felt—or at least hoped—we would one day become friends.

I didn't know then that he would be the man to calm the turbulent sea that was sinking my life and set my sails for better things.

Over the next few years we exchanged letters, phone calls, and books we were fond of reading. From time to time we'd share a meal. He was a stickler for promptness, and at least once I tested his patience by arriving late.

We'd meet in the small dining room of the Church Administration Building. The wooden fixtures and cozy atmosphere reminded me of the dining car on my train to Mexico. Sometimes his wife, Colleen, would join us. Together, it seemed to me, they formed two halves of the same orange.

Our conversations were filled with friendly thoughts about heavy matters.

"Colleen is so tenderhearted," Elder Maxwell once said when she was away from the table. "She's convinced the Rich Young Man in the parable went out, sold all he owned, and returned to follow the Savior." When he spoke about her, there was a soft sparkle in his eyes and voice.

At those lunches I came to realize that wives make us better than we are while never letting us believe we're better than we are.

When his wife was with him—or when Carol was with me—Elder Maxwell and I ate our vegetables dutifully. When they weren't along, we dug deep into the meat and potatoes.

We were husbands—except when the topic turned to spiritual matters. Then something magical happened. Elder Maxwell would turn a simple observation into a moment akin to William Blake's line about holding infinity in the palm of his hand and finding "eternity in an hour."

More than once I found eternity in those hour lunches with Elder Maxwell.

Like Thomas S. Monson's, Elder Maxwell's personal ministry was vast. He helped dozens along the strait and narrow. But he made each one of us believe we were the most important person he knew. Somehow, I don't know how, he actually felt that way when he was with us, and that made it so.

His letters to me always began with gratitude—"Just a note of appreciation," he'd write. Or, "Thanks, as always, for your kindness in sharing." "Thanks so much for your note, but even more for being my everlasting friend."

I wasn't writing about religion at the time. The jaunty little newspaper column I was publishing took a bemused stance before the world and tried to spin gold from straw. It was a "personality column." One woman at the paper said my ability to make something out of nothing impressed her. One editor said I was arrogant enough to think I could write myself out of anything—even prison. I wrote what the editors called "thumb-suckers." Still, Elder Maxwell read my column faithfully and often commented on it.

"I bet I read you more than you read me," he said at one point.

I didn't have a comeback. It was true. Religion had yet to take hold of me, and I didn't read LDS writing. I was living life between my beloved secular world and the fringes of the Church—the same place I'd been twenty years before. Elder Maxwell could see that. He felt the tensions. I know, at times, he could smell the alcohol on my breath at *Deseret News* functions.

But he never registered disappointment or played the scold. He hung with me. And my weary heart reached out to him.

Soon, just as surely as a cricket's chirp will change with the weather, the tone and voice of my column began sounding more reflective, more searching. A hint of religious longing began seeping from between the lines. And Elder Maxwell picked up on it. His spiritual gifts told him my heart of stone was turning—in Ezekiel's words—into a heart of flesh. And after one of our light-hearted lunches, instead of bidding me farewell, he asked me to come with him to his office.

Elder Maxwell's office was more like a den than an office. He had a drawing from one of his grandkids on the wall, along with the original painting of Joseph weeping in Liberty Jail by Liz Lemon Swindle. In typical fashion, I think he loved them both equally. A dynamic bust of the Savior stood on the top shelf of a glass case. There was also a small table and a couple of chairs where it appeared he did most of his work and interviewing. The big desk put too much wood and distance between him and those he wanted to counsel.

He got out some photographs and asked me to sit down with him. They were photos of Oliver Cowdery's original handwritten text of the Book of Mormon. The pages were just as we'd been taught—no corrections, no punctuation, and they had been written, it seemed to me, in a flurry, as if Oliver and the Prophet were up against a celestial deadline.

That thought chilled me a little. I knew Elder Maxwell himself was up against a deadline. He was battling one of the uglier forms of cancer. When he walked, he had to move slowly, which seemed to frustrate him. He knew there was still much to get done.

After a few moments with the photos, he got up, walked to the front wall, and stared at a photograph of grass and sand. It was a picture of Okinawa, where he had fought as a young soldier.

He said, "Sometimes, when I feel discouraged, I look at this and I say to myself, 'You did Okinawa, kid. You can do cancer.'"

Since being diagnosed, Elder Maxwell had begun a full-tilt ministry to other cancer patients. He felt he could help because he understood.

He returned to the table and took the chair closest to me.

"The other day I met with a woman," he said. "She not only has cancer, but her son has it as well. And you know, Jerry, there is not one drop of guile in her, not one."

When I looked at him he had tears in his eyes.

Sympathy tears sprang into mine. Elder Maxwell was the exact same way, but he didn't seem to realize it.

"Where do people find that kind of goodness?" I asked.

"I don't know," he said. "They must bring it with them, as baggage, from the preexistence—a good kind of baggage."

That's when my heart began to split apart.

That was my moment of "mighty change."

I've looked back at those few minutes in Elder Maxwell's office often since that day. And being analytical by nature, I've tried to pinpoint what happened to me.

The doctrinal explanations are pretty much straightforward. After all those years I'd finally allowed the Holy Ghost to come in out of the rain. I'd opened my heart to the workings of the Spirit.

But it was the feeling that such a "mighty change" triggered in me that intrigues me. I felt as if I had gotten in touch with a "deeper me," a self more profound and real than my day-to-day self—the self that eats, jokes, works, and sleeps.

Yes, my heart had been broken. But not the way romance gone bad breaks a heart. It was more as if my heart had been broken open—like a pomegranate—and gushed with overflowing sweetness.

It had been broken open like a piñata, spilling out its treasures.

It had broken and revealed something warm and alive—like a brittle egg giving way to the chick or a tightly wrapped cocoon bursting to free the butterfly.

I felt like a child who had left his swaddling clothes behind to go about his Father's business.

Earlier, I spoke of the great religious fantasy writers who moved their characters from the work-a-day world into the world of the Spirit by having them slip through a wardrobe or slide through a looking glass.

I realized, then, that's just how it works.

We move from the Kingdom of the World into the Kingdom of God by moving to a different room within us. Like those kiddy trinkets where the picture changes as you tip it back and forth in the light, we find the Kingdom of God by catching the light in a fresh, surprising way. Suddenly, we see all things as they really are. Our true hearts await us just beyond the looking glass. That was Paul's image, too—the "glass," the mirror, where we see things darkly but will eventually see them in full.

That day in his office, I told Elder Maxwell everything—how the sands inside of me had been shifting. I told him of my leaving Carol and my return. I told him how I was trying hard to "relearn the dance of Mormonism"—I believe that's how I put it. I had not just been wayward, I had been way wayward.

He seemed to have guessed as much. But he didn't want to know the details. He didn't want me to dwell on where I'd been. He was more interested in where I was going. And he worked to keep my mind on the prize.

"Have you and Carol thought about being sealed in the temple?" he said.

"Thought, yes," I said. "But that's about it."

"If you decide it's what you want," he said softly, "I'd be honored if you'd let me do it—that is, if I'm still well enough."

The tears flowed and flowed.

In Corinthians, Paul says that without charity, he was just "sounding brass or a tinkling cymbal." Some Bible commentators claim he was talking about "the noisy gong" in the pagan temples of Dionysus.

But I think Paul's image had a literal side.

As I drove home to Brigham City the day of my meeting with Elder Maxwell, everything without a spiritual element had a rattling quality to it. The callers on the talk radio stations sounded like tin foil in the wind. The pop songs felt cheap and tinny. The difference between the Spirit and the secular world was the difference between a cathedral bell and a toy piano.

I had tears in my eyes most of the way home. Yet through those tears, I could see behind the surface of things. I felt the goodness of the earth rolling along beneath the asphalt. I watched the red sunset in the west warm the peaks to the east with a rose-colored glow. They seemed to be glowing in empathy for their Western brethren. I sang to myself, as I often do. And my voice felt relaxed and free. Objects I looked at would hold my gaze. My attention didn't flit to and fro like a hummingbird's.

When I got home and began walking to the front door, Carol came to meet me. I knew she would see my puffy face and think something tragic had happened. She'd think my son, Ian, had been in a terrible accident or that I had found out I had just two days to live.

She greeted me and looked into my eyes.

"Oh, good!" she said. "Good!"

Since that day, I have come to view my time with Elder Maxwell as the gold standard for my personal spiritual experiences. I've returned to it a hundred times. And I've come to embrace that division inside of us between the Kingdom of the World and the Kingdom of God. We move into God's realm by passing through a veil of sorts, we must "leave the world." And whenever I leave the world to enter the Kingdom of God, I wonder why in the world I ever stayed away. In God's Kingdom we are given gifts piled high. We feel generous and kind. We feel called to do good things and feel the desire to share what we've felt. We become authentic, just as my little doppelgänger Pinocchio eventually became a real boy. We see past the obvious and into the essence of life.

And none of it is our doing. It is the Spirit at work within us. For all of our feelings of grace and goodwill we are dependent on God for our awakening—as we are with everything else.

Carol and I were sealed by Elder Maxwell on October 9, 1998. He was in all-out combat against his illness at the time. He'd lost his hair to chemo and the medications had added to his weight. He walked in slow motion, like a man wading through the shallow end of a swimming pool. We moved the sealing to a lower room in the Salt Lake Temple because he couldn't climb the stairs.

Besides Carol, Elder Maxwell, and myself, the only ones there were the two witnesses pulled from the ranks of the temple workers. That was my request. If we'd allowed others to attend, I knew I would regret having to leave too many others out. Besides, I felt Carol and I needed the moment to be just our own.

Elder Maxwell asked us questions about our life together and our plans. He taught us about temples from the scriptures and said his interpretation should not be mentioned beyond the temple walls. Then he offered his apostolic blessing, blessing us that our love would deepen, that we would find new insights and applications in the scriptures, and that we would "weather the squalls and storms in life."

Later, Carol would say each time he extended his hands to speak she felt an urge to slip her head beneath them.

When he delivered the key words of the ordinance, he was weak, but his voice was strong and resonant. His gaze fixed and true. I recognized both as hallmarks of the Spirit.

Because he was so spiritually robust, we could never know the physical toll that performing the sealing ordinance took on him.

By the grace of God and good medicine, Elder Maxwell would live on for another four and a half years. When he died on July 21, 2004, tributes from friends, colleagues, Church members, and a full battalion of former prodigals he had led back home filled the airwaves and the publications.

On the 24th of July, a fitting date, I wrote and published my own farewell to him in my column. I was moved and thrilled when President Monson would read from the column as part of his eulogy at Elder Maxwell's funeral.

* * *

Deseret News, July 24, 2004

*I once told Elder Neal A. Maxwell that I thought The
Church of Jesus Christ of Latter-day Saints was like a John
Deere tractor. It sputtered at times and threw a little oil, but it
kept chugging along, bringing in the sheaves.*

He thought that over a moment.

*"And sometimes," he said, "shocks of wheat fall from the
wagon."*

*It was typical Elder Maxwell. I was looking for a way to
excuse the Church for any perceived failings.*

He was looking for the souls who had fallen away.

Years ago, he looked and found me.

*Along with dozens of others, I'm one of Neal A. Maxwell's
"prodigals." I was floundering in the surf of the world when he
beamed a light my way, extended his hand, and pulled me to
shore.*

*When I first met him, I was a bit of a rounder. He was
serving on the* Deseret Morning News *board of directors. And
since we both approached the world "through language," we
would sometimes meet for lunch to exchange books and metaphors. The last time my wife and I met with him, his little
volume of religious thoughts had just come out. He called them
"blobs" and said the book was just a "mild sedative."*

*"I don't know if I'll write another full-length book," he
said. "My mind is like Swiss cheese. I feel like that cartoon
where the doctor shines a light in the patient's left ear and you
can see it shining out of the right one."*

*He said he felt he was now "coasting in for a landing,"
that he could "see the rooftops" beneath him.*

*Thursday, we learned Elder Maxwell had finally "touched
down."*

*Much has been said and written about his life in the past
couple of days. Much more will be said and written. Everyone
has his own version of him. I always saw him as a consecrated
soul. Many promise to consecrate their time and talents to*

God. But more than anyone I've known, Elder Maxwell did just that. He gave the impression that his intellect, energy, and wit belonged to God. He seemed to embody a short prayer uttered by Saint Augustine:

"Lord, let me offer you in sacrifice the service of my thoughts and my tongue; but first, give me what I may offer you."

That was how Elder Maxwell thought and lived.

As for all those hours he spent with me, I have no idea why I was singled out for such a blessing. I feel like the construction worker named Terry who visited the paper to talk about heart transplants. He'd received an implanted defibrillator. When that failed, he applied for and got a new heart. He was doing very well.

"I know you're asking, 'Why this guy?'" Terry said. "I ask myself that every day. I'm nobody special. I have no idea why God has granted me such favors."

Personally, I think God granted Terry such favors to show that he loves every person equally. It wasn't that Terry was "nobody special." It was that, in God's eyes, everybody is special. When it came to transplanting hearts, God didn't play favorites.

That was how Elder Neal A. Maxwell made people feel. There were no kings and paupers in his world, no castes or classes. There were only pilgrims—some who'd found their way, some who hadn't.

I was a wandering pilgrim when he first met me.

Without a second thought, he took me by the hand.

And with that simple gesture, he saved my life.

* * *

I miss Elder Maxwell.

In the following years, my wife would always refer to my return to the Church at his hand as my "first rescue." But eighteen months after our temple sealing, I would need a second rescue—this time a mortal rescue.

I didn't know it as I mourned the passing of Elder Maxwell.

And I didn't know it as I sat in my Miami hotel reliving the arc of my life on my way home from Bolivia. But a great chasm was opening up beneath me.

At the Cochabamba temple dedication I'd never felt more alive in my life. But within a matter of hours after leaving Miami and flying to Dallas, while boarding a plane home to Salt Lake City, I would collapse at the gate and my heart would stop beating.

In the blink of an eye, I was gone—my heart buckling in cardiac arrest.

In short, I was soon to die.

CHAPTER TEN:
The Luckiest Man Alive

THE NEXT MORNING IN MIAMI I still hadn't filed my column about the temple dedication for the paper. I decided to write it on the plane to Salt Lake City. I didn't want to break the mood. I felt wonderfully content. My son, Ian, was graduating from college in three days. My wife and I were doing well, and—professionally—I had a job that most journalists would die for.

I felt I'd finally climbed Kilimanjaro.

But I needed to brush up on my Shakespeare. Everyone knows when you're on top of things in a Shakespeare play, you're on your way down. And I'd soon slip toward the abyss.

For the moment, however, all I knew was I felt tired, elated, and a bit rushed to make the flight to Dallas and then back home. And my two years' supply of antacid was doing nothing to ease the pain in my chest.

I caught the flight to Dallas.

The Dallas airport prided itself on being an international hub. The problem was the airline gates were out on the ends of the spokes. On connecting flights you needed a plane just to get to your plane. And I arrived with little time to spare.

By hopping shuttle trains and running on escalators, I made it to American Airlines gate C25 as the last passenger was boarding. My chest ached and I was panting and sweating, but I handed the flight attendant my boarding pass as I tried to catch my breath.

Suddenly, the world grew fuzzy, tilted to one side, then faded slowly to white.

As I fell the man behind me caught me and asked, "Are you diabetic?"

"No," I said. "No."

Those would be my dying words.

If what happened to me then internally can be trusted, everything we've read about dying is true.

There was a bright light—burning like a bulb above an operating table. And yes, there was a sense of peace and well-being. What was happening to me felt very natural. I was dying. And dying was not terrifying. I recall wishing I had time to explain that to my wife and kids. I wanted them to know dying was not a bad thing. It was a normal thing.

I also discovered that God is a sleight-of-hand artist. The people watching me thought I had disappeared. But I hadn't. Like a master magician, God had slipped me from one hand to the other while no one was looking.

I was there. And I was gone.

Dead souls are palmed coins in the hand of God.

As for the Creator Himself, I'm convinced the teachings about our mortal lives being a separation from Him are also true.

Dying doesn't feel like starting on a new journey.

It feels like circling back home. Life and death are part of an orbit—like the sun, moon, and stars.

Eternity is, in fact, one eternal round.

In Dallas, my soul gathered itself and prepared to leave or, better, prepared to loop back like a racehorse to where it had begun. My spirit moved toward the door on the back wall of sleep.

Death takes place on the other side of sleep. It is a waking to another world.

The Japanese have it right. The color of death is white, not black. Death isn't a black hole, it's a channel of light as warm and soft as a birth canal.

Channels, I would later come to believe, were the way God went about His business.

Death and birth are the Grand Canals. And all other channels are versions of it. The body channels its food and waste, blood and breath. Conception and birth work through channels.

God works through channels when He gives messages to His prophets, who pass them on to us, through channels.

He wants us to be clean and unclogged so we can keep the Spirit "flowing."

The Spirit, I realized, wasn't a faucet you turn on or turn off. The Spirit was constantly flowing. And we can choose to block its flow or help it along.

We can be either an open conduit for it or a closed one.

Like jumper cables, we exist to pass along the current of God's will and love.

Meanwhile, back at the terminal gate, mortals were working hard to bring me back. And after a few minutes I could feel myself being tugged to the surface—pulled up and in, like the video of a baby's birth run in reverse.

I was a grain of sand getting sucked back into the upper chamber of the hour glass.

I felt I was rising through cool water. I believe if I'd kept my eyes open while being baptized, I would have felt the same thing then.

I saw shimmering images above me. They formed a circle. Were they angels?

No. They were concerned people, my first responders.

My eyelids fluttered.

"He's alive!" one man shouted.

His words made me feel like the Frankenstein monster.

I knew I had fallen, and maybe even fainted. I thought I'd been gone a couple of seconds. As I came around I groped for my camera bag. I couldn't miss my flight. I had that column to write.

"What are you doing?" someone asked.

"Getting on the plane," I said.

Someone else laughed.

"I don't think so," a female voice said.

Over the next few days I would learn the whole story. While I'd been floating around inside of myself, chaos had exploded around me. I'd grounded two flights and caused more commotion than a mad bomber. Newspapers and lunch wrappers were everywhere.

I vaguely remembered the mess. I vaguely remembered a man pointing to a bag on a bench where a custodian was cleaning. "Hey," he barked, "that's my burrito!"

It must have happened. I wouldn't invent a line like that.

The man behind me in line, the one who'd caught me, was Utah Grizzlies hockey star Taj Melson.

The woman who'd shocked me back to life with a pair of paddles was a flight attendant named Kelly Griffin. While others shouted, "Shock him! Shock him!" She had waited patiently for the machine to give her the order. When the command to shock came, POW!!

That's when I came floating back to the surface.

Other medical professionals soon joined the fray—Dr. Ronald A. Stoddard, Rufino Rodriguez, and Andrea Driggs, all from the grounded flight heading back to Utah. The paramedics were summoned. My memory of what happened next is full of scrambled images, like a corrupted video.

I see paramedics rolling me onto a gurney and running me to an ambulance. Young guys. Pumped with adrenaline. I see Kelly running beside me asking for my wife's telephone number. I hear one of the paramedics saying, "Right now you're the luckiest man alive."

Later he'd ask me to pick some lottery numbers for him to play.

At the emergency room of the Baylor hospital, a squadron of nurses flew into action, surprised to see I was still conscious. The pastor who served as the hospital chaplain came by. I have no idea how he got there so quickly. He asked if he could say a prayer for me.

"By all means," I said.

I was quickly bustled into the ICU and tests were started. I felt like the people who claim to be abducted by UFOs, where they get probed and prodded.

I soon decided those people weren't abducted by UFOs.

They were abducted by hospitals.

Later in the day a doctor came in to see me. He was all business.

"We're hoping you have a blocked artery," he said.

"Thank you," I said.

He didn't smile.

"If you don't have a blocked artery," he explained, "then we have an electrical problem. And that will be harder to deal with."

I did, thankfully, have a blocked artery. And it would require a triple bypass.

I remember thinking, *So much for the "acid reflux."* I thought of all the money I had wasted on antacid.

I also caught a break. My surgeon was top of the line—a fly fisherman, Dr. Busch, from Montana. I don't know if he tied his own flies, but if he did, I'm sure he included all eight eyes. He was that steady and dedicated.

They wheeled me into surgery, told me to work hard to get off the breathing apparatus because being on the machine too long had been known to make people a little daffy and dumb when they aged.

I've been convinced for years that I didn't get off the thing fast enough.

The anesthesiologist put me under his spell, then I went under the knife.

The Johnston line has had so much heart disease over the years that I'm surprised I didn't have some kind of genetic memory of heart failures.

My grandfather, on Dad's side, died of heart disease before sixty-five.

Uncle Kent was taken in his fifties.

My mother had died of a heart attack just four years earlier. My father had a heart operation and my great-grandad Jesse T. Rees— who'll be drifting into this narrative before too long—had strode out on his porch in the middle of a winter night to die of heart attack, facedown in the snow, a Book of Mormon in his hand.

As for me, when I was ten, I had rheumatic fever, which swelled my heart to twice its size. I was on the crest of death and probably would have died if my mother hadn't toted me from room to room on her back instead of forcing me to walk.

When I recovered I had a heart murmur, and my heart would never quite be the same.

It didn't seem to matter about our age or size or habits—bad hearts did the Johnstons in. It's why I laughed out loud in a movie where Harry Dean Stanton plays a used car salesman.

"Does this car have a guarantee?" a customer asks him.

"You bet it does," Stanton says. "It has a lifetime guarantee—just like your heart."

As for the operation itself, I won't drag you through all the details, only to say I came through according to the prepared script, my heart's lifetime warranty still in force. They gave me a teddy bear to hug against my chest when I coughed so I wouldn't blow out all the stitches and wires. I caught myself wondering if living on was really worth all the pain and hassle. I kept thinking of how John F. Kennedy had died in Dallas, just a few blocks from where I was lying.

The medical miracle, needless to say, was astounding. Science is golden. But as I recuperated, I found the human miracles to be even more amazing—all those human connections and well wishes that softened and warmed my sterile surroundings.

New friends entered my life—some forever. Old friends checked in.

"New friends are silver," President Thomas S. Monson often said, "but the old are gold."

For a patient at death's door, pretty much all friends are platinum.

I've thought many times since of the day the Spirit (as Joseph Smith translated) lifted Jesus to the top of the temple and Satan came to tempt Him. "Cast thyself down," he said, "for it is written, He shall give his angels charge concerning thee: and in their hands they shall bear thee up."[11]

The Savior, of course, didn't take the bait.

But I had no choice.

I'd been pushed from a great height. And to my astonishment, angels came to bear me up. Human angels. Hundreds of them. That, for me, was a wonder of wonders.

The *Deseret News* flew my wife to Dallas. The local LDS bishop and his wife, Dennis and Debbie Blackerby, came by. And two missionaries told me they'd felt impressed to stop at the hospital because there was work to do there—Elder Aaron Watson and Elder Travis Sutton. They got there just in time to give me a blessing of peace of mind and full recovery before surgery.

"Is there anything else we can do?" Elder Watson asked.

"You do need some clothes," my wife said.

My shirt and pants had been destroyed in the medical melee. I wrote down my various sizes and handed the elders my credit card. They were soon back with shirts and pants.

"Only Mormon missionaries could walk into a store with another man's credit card and not have the salespeople bat an eye," Carol said.

The elders had wonderful taste—for youthful styles. For the next week or so I would be the hippest geezer in East Texas.

Those two elders will always remain in my heart.

As will Kelly, the American Airlines flight attendant. She came by each morning to bring me magazines and treats. After one of her visits, I said, "Kelly, why are you doing all this?"

"I'm trying to keep you off Delta Airlines," she said. Then she added, "If you die now, it would kill me."

She would be the one to take me to the airport the day I finally left for Salt Lake City. By luck, I was leaving from the same gate—C25—where I'd gone down in a heap. The déjà vu made me dizzy.

Kelly stood in line with me, waiting and crying.

"People are going to think we're breaking up," I said.

"No, they won't," she said between sobs. "They'll think, look at that woman sobbing her eyes out, and that guy with her won't even offer her a Kleenex."

I laughed. I didn't have a Kleenex. I offered my sleeve.

Several months later, the airline flew me back to Dallas for a special ceremony. Kelly would be the guest of honor, and was excited I would be there.

"Mr. Johnston's coming back to Dallas to visit," she told her stepson.

"Mr. Johnston?" he said. "Are we still doing that?"

That evening Kelly was given a crystal eagle and a golden lightning bolt to wear on her lapel. She thanked the Lord in her remarks for letting the defibrillator training "stay in this little blonde head."

The airline gave me an award, too—a glass plaque etched with the words, "To Jerry Johnston, for carrying on the chain of life."

I think it meant, "Mr. Johnston. Thank you for not dying on our airplane."

A couple of days after my surgery in Dallas I was allowed to take phone calls. These were pre-cell days, so the calls came to the big black phone at my bedside. My story had hit the wire services— more because a pro hockey star was involved than me, I suspect. But soon well-wishes were arriving from everywhere. I heard from family and friends all over Utah. Then the circle widened.

I got a call from Allen Turner in Wyoming, my Young Men leader in Brigham City when I was fifteen years old.

I heard from the in-laws of my former in-laws in Mexico City.

Elder Neal A. Maxwell called, his voice flowing over me like the balm of Gilead. Just hearing him hastened the healing of my heart. He complimented me for speaking in such a happy voice. Looking back, I think it was the tranquilizers talking.

The phone wouldn't stop. I was busier than a telethon worker. I'd just fielded two calls when a third came ringing in.

"Hello?" I said.

"Jerry?" the voice on the other end said.

"Yes?" I said.

I waited.

"Jerry," the voice said, "did I give you that heart attack when I asked you to speak in the Cochabamba temple?"

CHAPTER ELEVEN:
Nuclear Family Chain Reaction

HEARING PRESIDENT HINCKLEY'S VOICE STARTLED me so much I dropped the phone. After his call I phoned my wife and dropped the phone on purpose as a test, just to be sure I hadn't punctured the prophet's eardrum.

She said she hardly noticed.

I assured President Hinckley he wasn't to blame for my predicament—that a lifetime of sitting around eating pizza was the culprit.

He made a knowing sound.

I told him the doctors in Utah had misdiagnosed my heart disease. They thought I had acid indigestion.

He found that less amusing.

Then I tried to fill him in, as quickly as I could, on the whole saga—my collapse at the airport, the whirlwind ride to the hospital, the operation, and the aftermath.

"You must feel very fortunate," he said.

"I do," I said. "Very fortunate."

Later, I thought about him choosing the word *fortunate* instead of *blessed*. Saying someone was "blessed" would seem natural for a prophet. But then I remembered the man Jesus had healed and told not to make too much of it. Instead, in one of my favorite King James phrases, the scriptures tell us, "But he went out, and began to publish it much, and to blaze abroad the matter."12

The man Jesus healed saw himself as a celebrity. If the prophet had told me I had been singled out and blessed, a guy like me just might start seeing himself not only as "blessed" but as "bless-ed"—God's Special Project, declared so by the prophet.

I've never known anyone who was more cautious and correct with his language than President Hinckley. He seemed to feel every nuance of every word.

As it was, I was having a hard time getting my head around the good fortune God had sent my way. Nor could I understand why it came to me and not someone else. I had been spared—either by design or luck of the draw—but why? And what about the hundreds of others with families and responsibilities who died of heart attacks each day while I healed away in the hospital?

I decided the only attitude that made sense was gratitude. Thankfulness, pure and simple. Anything else seemed to be over-reaching. Maybe this wasn't about me. Perhaps I had been rescued to play a role in the rescue of someone else. Perhaps I would still die on the flight back to Utah.

I saw that any feeling beyond gratitude had a hint of self-importance to it. If we tried to imagine godly motives behind our every breath, before long we'll want "little tabernacles" made in our honor.

I decided gratitude was the only viable point of view. And I would try to make it the basis of my salvaged life.

A few days later, I returned home, where I'd be greeted by months of cardiac rehab, a $40,000 implanted titanium defibrillator, and weeks of bed rest.

I finally returned to work in June. The column I wrote my first day back—the first piece I'd published since the one I wrote before heading for Bolivia—had a lot to say about gratitude.

A few weeks later the editor of the *Church News* asked me to write an extended first-person piece about my life-and-death, death-and-life experience.

I wrote the following.

* * *

Church News, 2000

> *Last spring I was sent to Bolivia, my old mission field, to cover the dedication of the Cochabamba Temple for the* Church News.
> *I departed as a "Happy Wanderer," off on an adventure. I ended up like the "Poor Wayfaring Man of Grief."*
> *Still, the real story is not about me at all.*
> *The real story is one of Christian love.*

The piece concluded:

> *Today, looking back, what would seem on the surface to be a wonderful experience (the temple dedication) followed by days of anguish were not that at all. In fact, the feeling of grace that came my way in the hospital was akin to my feelings in the temple.*
> *God was good and gracious.*
> *Christ was with us.*
> *The fellowship of the saints was sweet and powerful.*

* * *

Several weeks after getting back to work, I was having lunch with Elder Maxwell when President Hinckley came into the dining room. He stopped at our table.

"I'm on my way to South America," he said to me. Then flashing the twinkle that people loved, he said, "You want to come along?"

My heart didn't miss a beat.

"When do we leave?" I said.

I was dead serious.

I feel the same today.

I'd do it all again.

In the months after my recovery, I would learn that dying alters the way a person sees the universe. I didn't need to tell myself, "I almost died, I have to be more patient, I have to think long term."

Those shifts in attitude simply happened by themselves.

I also grew more fearless.

My father would be the first to tell you that, as a boy, I feared everything. I'd hold my ears when guns were fired and would refuse to climb tall ladders. Just the thought of being stiff-armed in a football game made my nose bleed. I said earlier that I fell in love with baseball. And I did. I fell in love with the lore, strategy, personalities, and history of the game. I tried to play but was so afraid of getting hit by pitches at the plate that I seldom got a hit. My batting average in Pony League was the same number as my school locker—125.

But after my dance with death, I became bolder, less jumpy, less easily cowed. And my quick impatience at others began to disappear.

I no longer got annoyed when my stepdaughters left the lights on or forgot to close the silverware drawer.

When people were late or kept me waiting, I no longer took it personally. Making a fuss over such matters was telling other people, "I'm more important than you. My time is more valuable than yours."

And I no longer believed that.

In short, I could feel my spirit begin to broaden and deepen.

I had learned, firsthand, how fragile we all were. We were like panes of glass. We could stand up against the wind and rain, the cold and the ice, but a pebble the size of a pea could shatter us.

And having been given a "delay en route," to borrow a phrase from Elder Maxwell, I threw my attention into the thing that would give me the most joy, fulfillment, and stability.

I put my attention on family.

We all say family is the most important thing in our lives. We all believe it. But not that many live it. Now, I was determined to live it. I would focus on not just my immediate family, but family past and family future, family telescoped out to form—in my mind—a long balancing pole to help me walk the high wire of life. And my attention quickly fell on one ancestor in particular, the last, true patriarch of our clan, my maternal great-grandfather,

Jesse Thomas Rees. My long line of chosen fathers was finally beginning to lead back home.

I became a student of his life and times. He died when I was still a little boy, yet I had fleeting memories of the old gent and his white mustache. He spoke in a Welsh accent and had a soft spot for Rudyard Kipling's *Jungle Book.* He wrote wonderful letters. He was a hard-nosed farmer, but he tilled the earth with a gentle heart.

I asked around the family and learned he wore a suit and tie whenever he'd listen to General Conference on the radio. He wore a tie to umpire baseball games. He believed in being—and looking—proper.

When a second cousin brought me a copy of his missionary journal, I dug into it like a mystery novel.

One of the first things Granddad Rees recorded in his journal was the blessing he'd received on August 10, 1898 as a new missionary. It was a high-minded and mighty blessing.

"You shall have great joy and rejoicing," the blessing said of his mission.

Granddad did.

"You shall travel by land and by water, upon the railroads and upon the thoroughfares, and your guardian angel shall have watch concerning you."

All that happened as well.

"You shall be warned of danger in time to escape."

Yes, he had been. Several times.

"Go forth happy and contented, glorifying the name of your Father," he'd been admonished, "realizing that you are not a martyr to the cause of Christ, but that you have been blessed of the Lord in being privileged to go forth as a messenger of life and salvation."

It would be how Granddad would live his life.

The blessing was given to him by J. Golden Kimball.

Yes, *that* J. Golden Kimball.

Today in the Church, "Uncle Golden" is used for comic relief. He was the General Authority who cussed and complained and whose barbed wit kept people in stitches. But in that blessing to my great-grandfather, I saw another man. I saw a man who spoke with spiritual sway, a man not afraid to prophesy and instruct.

Someday, an LDS author will show us that "other" J. Golden, the General Authority who did more than make people chuckle. The leader who could move them to tears and then move them into action.

Perhaps I'll do it myself.

Granddad served throughout the Pacific Northwest, but most of his journal is set in Montana. And the new "me"—the guy trying to take the long view of his heritage—realized he needed to go there to see it firsthand—to stand where Elder Jesse Rees had stood and see what he had seen. If I was going to expand my inner horizons, I'd have to expand my outer horizons.

I called a photographer friend, Ray Boren. As a child, Ray had lost his own father, so I suspected he could easily understand my obsession with resurrecting a family patriarch. I began packing my bags. Soon the two of us were en route to Montana to find the ghost of Jesse T. Rees—the Montana missionary.

As we neared Kalispell, we came to a train crossing. The lights flashed, the bar came down, but no train appeared. Then the bar went back up.

"Ghost train," I said.

"Maybe your great-grandpa has decided to join us," Ray said.

We laughed, me a little more uneasily than Ray.

Much of the past in Kalispell, Montana, we found, had been preserved, so we soon located the landmarks Granddad had described. Many still had the same fixtures from a hundred years before. I was able to stand where he had stood, see what he had seen, and—at times—I thought I could even feel what he had felt.

We found the home of Michael Pueblo, the cattle baron who fed Elder Rees and his companion and talked with them long into the night. We even found the old dance hall where he'd preached on Sundays. But where, in the past, I would have chalked our findings up to happy coincidences and lucky bits of guesswork, now I could feel a current pulling us. The law of chance was giving way in my mind to other possibilities.

We read Granddad's journal as we went along. I smiled at his entries. He was just as focused on food in his journal as I'd been in mine. He loved food and he loved making literary references. He was always quoting from Sir Walter Scott and others. In fact, Granddad, too, had fancied himself a poet, just as I had. He sprinkled his journal entries with the dust of poetry. In elegant penmanship he described the landscape around Flathead Lake:

Advancing from the south along the east side of the lake, the scenery which is pretty throughout all this section of Montana, becomes grand and inspiring. The ravines become deeper, the crystal streams more numerous, the peaks higher and steeper until they are transformed into perpendicular walls, rugged cliffs and magnificent pinnacles.

He wrote in a breezy, natural voice, a conversational voice. He would have made an interesting newspaper columnist.

One New Year's Eve, instead of celebrating at a party, Granddad and three other elders stayed put at home and wrote poetry about the coming year. He copied the poems from each elder into his journal, declaring, "After writing the above, we're wondering if we aren't better poets than preachers."

My unvarnished bias pegged Granddad's poem as the best. It had several stanzas, including this one:

Good morning to you, Mr. New,
Gladly do I welcome you.
Before you extend the parting hand,
Take me to my kindred band.

As Ray and I drove about, I was slowly beginning to understand the man, the old country schoolteacher. In photographs, I could see the Welsh in his brown eyes as it reflected in my own. I sensed a kindred spirit in his writing—his choice of topics and words. I was getting to know him. My friend Clive Romney claims if we're going to turn our hearts to our fathers, we need more than a set of names. We need to learn about their lives. And by learning more about Granddad Rees, I was learning more about myself.

When we got back to Utah, I wrote a series of columns about the trip. Rees relatives from around the country soon responded by sending me photographs, letters, and—the real prize—a taped interview with Granddad. And with every new piece of his life that came in, I felt more at home in the world.

I also unearthed a nugget of spiritual truth.

If it's true the sins of one soul can be handed down for generations, it is also true the virtues and qualities of character can be passed along as well. And I could see a chain of Granddad's traits coming through others down to me.

Who he was, what he felt, how he lived was with me every day because his children and grandchildren had passed his legacy along to me in their lives. And I was obliged to keep the chain going.

In the years since a heart attack turned my heart to my fathers, I've come to think of family historians as nuclear scientists. They are following a chain reaction of training and qualities that has come to them in their blood and bones.

Granddad Rees's biggest influence on my life did not come from his journals or poems, but in the way he shaped the life of his daughter—my grandmother. She was raised in his image. Then she went about raising her daughter in that image, who would raise me the same way.

The world called my grandmother "Floss," but for us she was always "Nanny Flo." When she was a girl, she fell from a horse and was left with a mangled left hand, which she always carried in the pocket of her apron. She did everything one-handed. But we kids never noticed. She painted, cooked, cleaned, drove the tractor during hay season, and sewed clothes.

My mother, with her two good hands, would emulate her, picking fruit and gathering eggs one-handed. She thought it was the family's way.

Like Great-Granddad, Nanny Flo had a gentle, clever wit.

Like Granddad Rees, she was a first-rate storyteller and wrote poetry.

Her stories are the reason I became a writer.

When I'd show up at her little farmhouse to be quarantined with the chicken pox, measles, or mumps, she'd read to me from Kipling's *Jungle Book,* which her father had read to her. She pumped me full of Kipling's cherished Victorian ethics—a strong mind in a strong body, a stiff upper lip, and all of Mowgli's famous "laws of the jungle" that found their way into the Boy Scouts and the early Mormon Church.

My grandmother didn't have to work hard to pass along the "Rees way." My mother happily patterned her own life on everything my grandmother did.

In the years since my death in Dallas, I've tried hard to pattern my own attitudes on hers.

Family. It's the vital element that makes all of life's other ingredients "set up" and jell.

The day of Mom's funeral, a family friend poked his head in the window of our coach and said, "A good life makes for a good funeral."

Somebody had said something similar at my grandmother's funeral.

And my mother's funeral was truly memorable for us all.

At the viewing, each person shared something Mother had said to them. It was as if she'd sewn a gold coin into each of their jackets.

"She told me I had Santa Claus eyes," one old man said.

"She told me not to tell her how long she had to live," a doctor said, "because she'd be sure to die then just so I wouldn't feel embarrassed."

"When I had my baby girl," a woman said, "she sent me a tiny pair of red, patent-leather shoes."

Tiny red shoes began showing up in the flower arrangements. We soon realized they were her signature gift, but we bumbling boys had never noticed.

When writer Henri Nouwen's mother died, he sent a letter to his father in Holland, saying, "If, however, Mother's life was a life for us, we must be willing to accept her death as a death for us . . . To say it even more drastically: we must have the courage to believe that her death was good for us and she died so that we might live."13

I saw that phenomenon at work. Many things Mother tried to accomplish in life she was only able to accomplish with her death.

The family was finally together—at the funeral—as she'd wanted us to be for decades.

Tensions among us were broken down. Peace offerings were made.

. Her two wayward grandsons not only ended up inside a church but arrived in white shirts and ties—pallbearers for her casket.

My father's steely distance was finally broken, and he was able to touch, for the first time in decades, the tender part of his heart.

She's always wanted that.

And me?

My wife and many others are convinced my mother led me back to the Church from her place in the spirit world. It was something she tried to do on earth for years without success.

Today—in my postcardiac world—I'm constantly trying to "shape" the lives of my children and grandchildren to reflect the lives and ideals of Great-Granddad, Nanny Flo, Mom, and others who've gone before.

One evening, while chatting with my son's wife, Amy, I asked about personality traits she'd noticed in my grandson Luke, a husky kid of two who is the firstborn son of a firstborn son of a firstborn son.

"He's a tease," she said.

That sounded familiar.

"And when he gets frustrated with something, he'll get mad and run away. But he'll eventually go back to it. He doesn't leave forever."

I knew the feeling.

"And he's very tenderhearted. Maybe too much so," she said.

I thought of a phrase I've used often: "Sometimes I'm too sensitive for my own good."

Granddad Rees could have jotted the same thought in his letters. He was that way. Grandmother could have put it in a poem, my mother in a letter, and my son could have easily sent it my way in a text. We were family members. We understood each other. That's because genetically and spiritually, we were each other.

Sometimes, I remember thinking, the circle of life is more than a circle. It's a spiral—like the wire binding on a notebook. It spins down through the generations repeating time and again the patterns forged by family members long before we came along. Turning our hearts to our fathers is easier than we imagine. In our marrow, they are already with us.

That's just one living lesson I received as a gift, for dying.

The long pole that helps us balance on life's high wire is family—family stretching into the future and far back into the past.

Family is the way we keep our footing.

Family is how we make it across the abyss to the other side.

And waiting for us on the other side is what my philosopher friend would call "the Platonic ideal of all fathers."

God our Father.

I'm almost embarrassed that learning that little insight—that God is the Father I always wanted—took me so many years. The list of mortal men I've shuffled into the role of "surrogate father" would fill a small phone book. And the qualities I responded to in each of them—the things that made me want to "fatherize" them—were the virtues God had been holding out to me all along: warmth, patience, interest, concern, protection, and love.

I wrote earlier that I once spoke at a Sunday meeting for women prisoners. That day, I asked how many of them had been betrayed by a man. Every hand went up.

Then I pointed to the solitary painting of Christ on the wall.

"He will never do that to you," I said.

"When you want to try your wings, He won't criticize or hold you back, He'll help. When you talk to Him, He'll listen for hours without scolding. When you just want someone to be nearby, He'll be there."

Today, I think I can relate to women who've told me they had been so badly betrayed by a man they found it difficult to make themselves vulnerable to God, another man. I struggle with such things. The emotional chilliness and neglect I felt when I was a boy lead me, today, to still approach God at times "on little cat's feet," to borrow from Carl Sandburg. And when I feel He has overlooked me, I catch myself thinking, "So what else is new?" I'd like to say, with Paul, that I have "run the good race," but I can't. I'm still on the backstretch, struggling.

Still, the fact that in six decades God has always shown up when I've shown the courage to look for Him tells me something. It tells me He won't quit on me. That I may well be a work in progress, an odd-shaped bowl on His potter's wheel, and the Potter is determined to get me right.

I spent my life looking for a father when the best was right at my elbow all the time.

Now, I continue to learn how to make myself open up to whatever He has to offer.

That might sound like a good place to end a book like this—a young boy goes looking for a father and comes full circle to find he had the most wonderful father possible with him all along. But life is seldom that tidy. So there's no reason books should be. The truth is, I had at least one thing more to learn about fatherhood and fathers.

In his April 2002 Conference talk, Elder Jeffrey R. Holland spoke about the Parable of the Prodigal Son. He stressed the part in the story played by the second son—the envious son—and he cautioned about falling into the trap of resentment.

But it would be his comments about the father—not the sons—that caught my attention.

"The tender image of this boy's anxious, faithful father running to meet him and showering him with kisses is one of the most moving and compassionate scenes in all of holy writ. It tells every child of God, wayward or otherwise, how much God wants us back in the protection of His arms."[14]

When the talk appeared in the *Ensign*, I checked the footnotes. I found Elder Holland had made a couple of references in his talk to my old "reading companion," Henri Nouwen and his book *The Return of the Prodigal Son.*

I had read the book several years before and had even shared a copy of it with Elder Maxwell. But after Elder Holland's talk, I went back to it and carefully digested it.

And I found the next move I had to make in this "eternal round" we call living. Nouwen writes the following:

> *The final stage of the spiritual life is to so fully let go of all fear of the Father that it becomes possible to become like him . . . every son and daughter has to consciously choose to step beyond their childhood and become father and mother for others.*
>
> *God's compassion is described by Jesus not simply to show how willing God is to feel for me . . . but to invite me to become like God and to show the same compassion to others.*[15]

I was already a father. I had raised a family. I had accepted that role and been dutiful about it. But I had never fully felt fatherly. In fact, when the chips were down, I saw myself as somebody's son. I would revert to being a boy and go looking for a father to help me out, to take me on as a project and teach me what I needed to know.

But I was aging quickly now. It was time "I put away childish things."

Instead of constantly being mentored, it was time for me to mentor.

My great-grandfather had held on to his childlike heart, the sweetness that kept him reading Kipling's *Jungle Book* well into his eighties. But he had been willing to become, heart and soul, the family patriarch. He didn't shirk from maturity.

Like Granddad, my son, Ian, was tenderhearted—sensitive to the point I'd seen him cover the ears of the cat when he said negative things about it. But he was working to be the man he was meant to be.

As for me, I still idolized twenty-year-old baseball players and, when nobody was looking, behaved like a boy bouncing on his parents' bed. Like many men, I'd held on to boyhood. And that was fine, to a point. But now I needed not to "find my inner child," but find my "inner father."

Fortunately, I knew someone who could show me how that was done.

He willingly had taken on the role of father to those in need.

It was time for me to understand what true earthly fathers were made of.

CHAPTER TWELVE:

Spiritual Grown-ups: Thomas S. Monson

I'VE KEPT A PHOTO OF the young Thomas S. Monson that I found among my mother's effects. I'm guessing he's thirty-five in the picture. And when I look at it, I realize he has been with me for most of my life.

He was called to be an apostle when I was still a young boy. He has been a voice in my ear for nearly fifty years.

His warm, gentle Conference talks were my mother's favorites.

"He tells stories," she would say, "stories about real people with real names in real places."

She enjoyed listening to the inflections in his voice and watching his facial expressions.

His style of speaking was always his own. To my ear, he often sounded like a caring father sharing stories with his children. He spoke through a smile, as if he were as much a child as a father.

He was both.

And he knew when to be each.

When I began writing for the *Deseret News* in 1978, President Monson was president of the board of directors at the paper. And over the years I'd slowly gotten to know him—not through the Church but through the "side door" of the *Deseret News*.

I am among the many who can witness to his kindness. When I'd write a column about someone close to him, he'd often drop me a note: "You captured the heart and essence of the man," he'd write. Or, "I have long admired the many qualities that you also observed."

When I was dropped by that cardiac arrest in Dallas, President Monson was spiritually among the first responders.

"How shocked I was to learn of the sudden illness that struck you on your way home from the dedication of the Cochabamba Bolivia Temple," he said in a letter. "I immediately placed your name on the prayer roll of the First Presidency and the Quorum of the Twelve."

I found myself wondering how many such letters I had sent. Or did I simply enjoy getting them?

I was still the needy son more than the giving father.

I would also learn that the number of people under President Monson's watchful eye could populate a small county. His hands were always filled and always extended.

And yet, perhaps since I had gotten to know him through the dry-eyes of professional journalism, I saw another side to the man.

I have seen President Monson raise himself to full height in defense of the Kingdom. I have seen the softness of his personal touch give way to a backbone fashioned from the Iron Rod, a stalwart quality that called to mind the prophets of old.

When, as God's spokesman, President Monson has felt called to protect the vulnerable, humble souls who populate the Kingdom, he has shown the fortitude of Ammon, or young David, as they stood between their masters' sheep and wily beasts and bandits.

I think, if I may be so bold, that that may have been how Jesus felt the day He cleansed the temple. The temple was the heart of His Father's Kingdom, but the money-grubbers had contaminated it. They had taken something that should have been rendered unto God and rendered it unto Caesar.

They had taken the Golden Rule and melted it into gold bullion.

How it must have pained the Savior to see the meek being swindled by the shysters. But perhaps it pained him more to see the temple—a refuge for the lost and weary—be turned into a common casino. It was the worst form of betrayal, the betrayal of God.

"It is written," he said, "My house is the house of prayer. But ye have made it a den of thieves."

Many times I have seen President Thomas S. Monson step into those shoes. He has been strong for those who lacked strength.

And yet, with spiritual resolve, he always stressed tenderness. He was a walking allegory of the way we should treat our brothers and sisters.

The young at heart in the Church responded to his youthful verve and—at times—his playfulness. But we all needed to look more closely. He was showing us how to stay young. But more than that, he was showing LDS men—me, in particular—how to be mature.

The week he became president of the Church, I welcomed him with a column:

* * *

Deseret News, February 7, 2008

> *For many people, President Thomas S. Monson is the LDS leader they can almost imagine addressing by first name. . . .*
>
> *No matter how many heads of state he will meet in his new calling as president, no matter how many national interviews he gives or how international his reputation becomes, LDS believers know part of him will forever be the young bishop from 50 years ago—the "ward healer" determined to elevate humanity one good deed at a time.*
>
> *For decades, President Monson was our "pastoral apostle."*
>
> *Now, he's our "pastoral president."*
>
> *And the thought brings feelings of warmth and well-being and security. . . .*
>
> *As I listened to President Monson speak at his press conference on Monday . . . in a moment of whimsy I remembered reading Superman comic books as a boy. I could never understand why the Man of Steel spent so much time chasing down cat burglars and tugging babies from the path of speeding*

cars. He could have cured cancer, fed Africa, found oil on Mars. Now, at age 59, I get the picture. In those early comics, Superman wasn't about pushing life as we know it to new heights. He was about teaching us how to lift others—how to elevate humanity "one good deed at a time."

It was, of course, the approach pioneered by the Greatest Teacher of them all. It's also an approach President Thomas S. Monson has modeled over a lifetime.

I know, in his new calling, President Monson will have less time to visit immigrants, single moms, and others. But I also know he would if he could. And that, somehow, is enough.

* * *

Over the years, President Monson has been wonderfully generous toward me. Some of his kindnesses have been tangible, like the leather-bound book he sent my way with a stirring inscription. Others have been simple moments that will live forever in my heart, as when—at the funeral of Elder Neal A. Maxwell—he chose to read from one of my columns in his eulogy.

But the gift that has mattered most to me is the one that all authentic men of God give freely to those willing to accept it.

It is the gift of perspective.

The prophet refuses to amass disciples. He will carry out his calling as leader and patriarch, but he has no interest in becoming a celebrated sage—as so many religious leaders do. Instead, he constantly points us beyond himself toward the heavens, where the true Master and Mentor resides.

As I've gone about my life, searching for a worthy mentor, a good master, a worthy father, I have spent decades running from the answer. Like the poet Francis Thompson, I've fled the Hound of Heaven, afraid it would devour me. I couldn't see the hound was a kind and caring Savior wanting to embrace me.

Earthly beings will disappoint us.

Humanity leaves us wanting.

Only deity is enough.

And like the loaves and fishes, the supply of God's love will never run out. Any quest that takes us in another direction may begin with gladness, but it is destined to end in despair.

Being a good son means learning how to become a good father.

And being a good father means pointing others away from ourselves and toward the only one who won't disappoint us—our Eternal Father.

Elder Neal A. Maxwell had gotten to that point of view long before I reached it. And he had described what he'd observed.

He said, "Discipleship in our day, as in all eras, has as a goal not our being different from other men, but our need to be more like God."

Amen, I say, to that.

CHAPTER THIRTEEN:
Ears Like a Man

I BEGAN THIS BOOK WITH the line, "While I write this, I keep looking out the window where the late evening clouds are as hard and gray as Grandma's old pewter dishes."

I bring it to a close tonight by saying, "While I write THIS, I'm suffering from a case of the heebie-jeebies."

I look back at these chapters and realize I've written intimate details about my life for strangers to read that no thinking man would show his best friend. Still, I feel I've been drawn to do it. The words for this book flowed freely, like those songs I sang in the car on my way home from my big moment with Elder Maxwell. My focus has been strong, but relaxed and natural. I've felt sweetness and peace. I've felt young. Such things, again, appear to be the calling cards of the Spirit.

Perhaps only fools wear their hearts on their sleeves. But when I find myself fretting about such things, I remember a story about Charles Ives the American composer. He was attending the premiere for one of his pieces. His compositions were challenging. Some found them infuriating. And that night was no exception. During the concert, the story goes, the audience began to hiss and boo. Ives, seated near the front, grew annoyed. Then angry. He stood and faced the crowd.

"Come on!" he shouted. "Use your ears like a man!"

By that, I think he meant, "Open up. Don't be defensive. Don't judge it. Expand yourself. Reach. Embrace. Feel!"

In other words, what he was saying to the crowd is what I've said to myself for decades and what I continually said to myself as I was writing this book.

Ives was shouting, "Come on! Use your heart like a man!"

It's a thought I try to keep near the front of my brain.

It's hard for me to think that more than ten years have passed since my heart-stopping moment in Dallas. As I said at the beginning, I'm sixty-two now. And—as I said—my life can be measured in even chunks. I remember reading once that every man's life has three stages: He believes in Santa Claus. He doesn't believe in Santa Claus. He is Santa Claus.

In my case you could probably substitute the words "a father" for "Santa Claus" and come pretty close.

It's 2011 now. Many of the people mentioned in this book have passed on. But more than a few are still with us. I hear from them from time to time—Elder Coleman sent me an e-mail not long ago. I assume he still drinks milk. Kelly Griffin was named Employee of the Year at American Airlines. I heard that Taj, the hockey star who rescued me at the airport, left the rink to study medicine. My friend Randall Hall is now a major cog in the wheel of Church education. As for the little grandmother who gave me a handkerchief for the Hosanna Shout in Bolivia and the paramedic who asked me for lottery numbers, I'd pay a thousand Bolivian pesos to know what they've been up to.

After everything that has happened, it seems odd to say that there are days I still see myself as a strange fit in the Church, though I think it's a strong fit—like Gary Cooper the Quaker in the film *Friendly Persuasion*. When people in the writing community—my professional community—ask why I returned to a church I had abandoned, I give them a writer's response. I point to C. S. Lewis and the years he wrestled with religion.

Lewis kept asking himself why everything that the world considered "imaginary"—miracles, God's grace, angels—were the very things that made him feel most alive, while the conventional view of "reality" left him cold, dark, and numb.

He went back and forth between the Kingdom and the World

until J. R. R. Tolkien, the "Hobbit master," took him aside and said, "Failure to believe, Jack, is just a failure of imagination."

With that, Lewis made the leap from the chilly world and submerged himself in the bright, vibrant reality of his heart.

I understand his choice completely. Being one of the dead burying the dead is not living.

That's the short answer for my "reversion" to religion. I've already given you the long answer in this book:

I got homesick for my Heavenly Father—and homesick for all He offers, asks, and is.

I got homesick for my tribe and my family, the people who made me what I am and gave me what I've gotten. In short, I got homesick for my true self.

Oh, I still get those old feelings of claustrophobia in the Church from time to time. Sometimes that white shirt and tie seem to fit a little too tight, and I hear the words of those in authority as the rumblings of generals. But I know those feelings will pass, and I will eventually slip back "through the spiritual looking glass" to find a place that is kind of a Cochabamba of the heart—an inner land of milk and honey that even migrating birds never bother to leave.

Finally, since God has been the Wagon Master of my haphazard and dusty trek through life, let me leave you with His words, not mine.

This scripture, I think, was Elder Maxwell's favorite. It's from the Book of Mormon, where Nephi is speaking with an angel. The angel asks Nephi if he's able to process all the fantastical, befuddling things God does.

"I do not know the meaning of all things," Nephi replies, but "I know that he loveth his children" (1 Nephi 11:17).

Writer Ian Frazier claims every book must have at its core one truth the writer sees as beyond dispute. In this book, I pray Nephi's reply to the angel is that truth.

NOTES

1   Sheri L. Dew. *Go Forward with Faith: The Biography of President Gordon B. Hinckley.* Salt Lake City: Deseret Book Company (1996), 306.

2   Dew, 306.

3   Dew, 307.

4   Henri J. M. Nouwen. *Gracias!* New York: HarperCollins (1987), 8–9.

5   Matthew 18:4.

6   Robert Louis Stevenson. "Thanks to Our Father," *A Child's Garden of Verses.*

7   Ernest Hemingway. "A Clean, Well-Lighted Place," *The Complete Short Stories of Ernest Hemingway.* New York: Simon & Schuster (1998), 291.

8   Loren C. Dunn. "Testimony," *Hymns,* No. 137.

9   John 11:35.

10 *2001 Church Almanac.* Salt Lake City: Deseret News.

11 Matthew 4:6.

12 Mark 1:45.

13 Henri J. M. Nouwen. *A Letter of Consolation.* New York: Harper & Row (1989).

14 Jeffrey R. Holland. "The Other Prodigal," April 2002 General Conference. As of September 9, 2011: http://lds.org/general-conference/2002/04/the-other-prodigal?lang=eng&query=Other+Prodigal.

15 Henri J. M. Nouwen. *The Return of the Prodigal Son: A Story of Homecoming.* New York: Doubleday (1994), 115.